JM

Jewish Music as Midrash:

What Makes Music Jewish?

D0901494

by Michael Isaacson

ISBN 13: 978-0-914615-36-1
ISBN 10: 0-914615-36-X

ECM Books and Music
4841 Alonzo Avenue
Encino, CA 91316

(818) 343-6450
eggcreamer@sbcglobal.net
www.MichaelIsaacson.com

First Edition, 2007

In conjunction with:
Isaac Nathan Publishing Co., Inc.
22711 Cass Avenue
Woodland Hills, CA 91364
(818) 225-9631

What Others Say . . . .

If anyone knows Jewish Music today it is Dr. Isaacson and this study is a testament to his prodigious knowledge and skill. This is a wonderful book.

—Rabbi Lawrence Kushner, author

Dr. Michael Isaacson's work is of the highest quality. This book extends that quality not just to music, but to writing about music. It is a genuine contribution to the field.

—Dr. Lawrence Hoffman,
Professor of Liturgy, Hebrew Union College

Michael Isaacson combines a life time of compositional know-how with an informed understanding of Jewish literary midrash to tackle the questions of authenticity and innovation in Jewish music. He offers us valuable tools with which to listen, understand, andremember much of the music that defines our Jewish lives. Dr. Isaacson's experiences creating effective dramatic music for live theatre, television and film come into play to clarify issues in worship music. *Jewish Music As Midrash: What Makes Music Jewish?* is a profoundly original book that has few models preceding it but is certain to set a course for sacred artistic studies well into the future.

—Samuel Adler, Professor of Composition,
Juilliard School of Music

Michael Isaacson's analytic observations of synagogue music past and present and his vast accomplishments in composing sacred, secular, and media music combine to offer the reader and listener a privileged view of where Jewish music has been, where it is today, and where it has the potential of developing in the future. This is a book that is sure to benefit Jewish and non-Jewish professionals, lay-persons, and all who are fascinated with the stimulating question "What, in fact, is Jewish music?" The two CDs of Isaacson's midrashic musical examples, which are included, are more than worth the price of the book alone."

—Rabbi Stephen S. Pearce, Senior Rabbi
Congregation Emanu-El, San Francisco

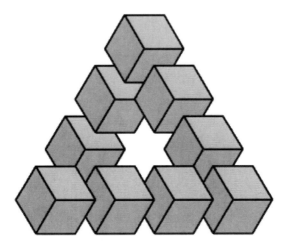

This *Magen David* (A Star of David), represents the Jewish spirit in the center of the most durable geometric shape—a triangle.

Yet, it is made from negative space, and *tsimtsum*—God's imploded presence. (Is it real or is it an illusion?). Surrounded by tenuously held together detached entities (as quantum physics and Kabbalah tell us we all are), its singular shape, though born in wonder, gives focus, unity, and hope to a world moving in ambiguous and conflicting directions. The image, a string theory visual metaphor, is also a beautiful visual example of the *midrash* of space.

—Chapter Eight, The *Midrash* of Space

Acknowledgments

> At times our own light goes out and is rekindled by a spark
> from another person. Each of us has cause to think with deep
> gratitude of those who have lighted the flame within us.
>
> —*Albert Schweitzer*

Music does not fall from the heavens like manna. It takes conscious awareness, ability, passion, concern, and nurturing to create. With thanks to our Creator, I wish to acknowledge all those in my life who have expressed and demonstrated their love and care, and have enabled me to reciprocate through the music that I have composed and for others' music, which I have written about and conducted.

To my treasured litany of parents, relatives, teachers, friends, colleagues, and critics who empowered me to grow, to those singular collaborators who consistently expended their very best efforts in the name of music, in general, and sacred music, in particular, to those magnificent souls who shared their best ideas and thought processes with me, guiding my heart and hand, and to the many who have listened to my music with open ears: I am grateful for all that I have been gifted and continue to learn from you.

Sincere thanks to all the fine artists who have, over the years, performed my music at services and concerts, and graced recordings of it with their commitment and talent. More than thirty of these many wonderful performances can be enjoyed on the companion CDs to this book.

I express my appreciation to all of my judicious friends who have meticulously read the manuscript of this book, offering both incisive and constructive criticism. Special thanks to David Epstein, Cantor Jay Frailich, and Barry Zwick for their literary considerations and to Nina Mayer for her skillful editing.

My love and gratitude to my wife Susan who gave me her priceless gifts of time and concentration, and to my sons Ari and Andy for passing their father's ideas forward to their generation.

Finally, my thanks to you, the reader, who, it is hoped, after a careful read and listen, may understand Jewish music in an invigorated and more meaningful way.

Baruch Atah Adonai Eloheinu Melech Haolam Shehechiyanu, V'kiy'manu, V'higianu Lazman Hazeh.

Praised be You, Eternal our God, Ruler of the Universe, who has kept us alive, sustained us, and permitted us to reach this moment in time.

—*Michael Isaacson, 2007*

Table of Contents

What sort of God would that be who has only one way in which
to be served?

— *Yaakov Yitzhak, quoted by Martin Buber, Way of Man*

Acknowledgments

Table of Contents

Recorded Illustrations on Companion CDs 1 & 2

Introduction

Chapter   1 - Mastering the Challenges of Listening 21

Chapter 2 - The Identifying Traits of Music 41

Chapter 3 – A Conundrum Wrapped in An Enigma:
  What Makes Music Jewish? 55

Chapter 4 - What is Traditional *Midrash?* 67

Chapter 5 - The *Midrash* of the Orchard 83

Chapter 6 - The *Midrash* of A Single Tone 97

Chapter 7 - The *Midrash* of Time 105

Chapter 8 - The *Midrash* of Space 117

Chapter 9 - The *Midrash* of Separation 127

Chapter 10 - The *Midrash* of Drama 137

Chapter 11 - The *Midrash* of Liturgical Music 171

Chapter 12 - The *Midrash* of Life Cycle Music 199

Chapter 13 - The *Midrash* of Wisdom Music 209

Chapter 14 - Listening with *Midrashic* Ears 227

Chapter 15 - Afterward 233

In memory of my grandparents:

Anna and Michael Zimmerman [z"l]

Sarah and Julius Isaacson [z"l]

Recorded Illustrations on Companion CDs 1 and 2

Jewish Music As Midrash:
What Makes Music Jewish?
by Michael Isaacson

It is good to make a habit of inspiring yourself with a melody…
For the loftiness of melody is beyond all measure.

—*Rebbe Nachman of Bratslav*

Chapter 1 - Mastering the Challenges of Listening
\# 1 *Nigun for Sabbath's Farewell* sung by Roslyn Barak .... 2'45" pg. 30
\# 2 *Yism'chu* sung by Faith Steinsnyder .... 1'43" pg. 33

Chapter 3 - What Makes Music Jewish?
A Conundrum Wrapped in an Enigma
\# 3 *Sheva B'rachot* sung by Aviva Rosenbloom .... 5'15" pg. 64

Chapter 5 - The *Midrash* of the Orchard
\# 4 *Hashkiveinu* sung by Faith Steinsnyder .... 4'28" pg. 92

Chapter 7 - The *Midrash* of Time
\# 5 *Oseh Shalom* sung by Herschel Fox .... 3'19" pg. 113

Chapter 8 - The *Midrash* of Space
\# 6 *Make Me A Sanctuary* sung by Jay Frailich .... 2'39" pg. 124
\# 7 *They Are Children* sung by Jerry Whitman .... 4'13" pg. 126

Chapter 9 - The *Midrash* of Separation
\# 8 *Havdalah Suite* sung by Roslyn Barak .... 18'00" pg. 133

Chapter 10 - The *Midrash* of Drama
\# 9 *Sh'ma* from *Hegyon Libi* sung by Roslyn Barak .... 1'44" pg. 154
\#10 *Ahavat Olam/Sh'ma* sung by Mark Childs .... 2'28" pg. 154
\#11 *B'ni* sung by Faith Steinsnyder .... 3'00" pg. 165
\#12 *Biti* sung by Faith Steinsnyder .... 2'49" pg. 167

Chapter 11 - The *Midrash* of Liturgical Music
\#13 Torah cantillation chanted by Michael Isaacson .... 30" pg. 177
\#14 Haftarah cantillation chanted by Michael Isaacson ..... 30" pg. 178

\# 15 *Esther the Queen* sung by Faith Steinsnyder .... 2'36" pg. 180
\# 16 Traditionally sung *V'ne-emar* .... 30" pg. 190
\# 17 Metrically correct *V'ne-emar* .... 30" pg. 190
\# 18 *Bayom Hahu* sung by Faith Steinsnyder .... 2'39" pg. 191
\# 19 *Adon Olam* sung by the Westminster Conservatory
       Youth Chorale, conducted by Dr. Frank Abrahams ... 3'10" pg. 194
\# 20 *Avinu Malkeinu* sung by Nathan Lam .... 3'25" pg. 195
\# 21 *L'Dor VaDor* sung by Jay Frailich .... 3'07" pg. 196
\# 22 *Hin'ni* sung by Faith Steinsnyder .... 3'54" pg. 197

Chapter 12 - The *Midrash* of Life Cycle Music
\# 23 *Nishama Shenatata Bi* sung by Faith Steinsnyder .... 3'21" pg. 202
\# 24 *The Covenant* - narrated by Morley Feinstein,
       sung by Jay Frailich .... 4'51" pg. 202
\# 25 *S'i Na Einayich* sung by Wally Shachet-Briskin .... 4'21" pg. 203
\# 26 *Sheva B'rachot* sung by Chayim Frenkel .... 3'18" pg. 205
\# 27 *This Quiet Dust* sung by Faith Steinsnyder .... 2'56" pg. 207
\# 28 *Enosh* sung by Faith Steinsnyder .... 3'38" pg. 207

Chapter 13 - The *Midrash* of Wisdom Music
\# 29 *Im Ein Torah* sung by Nathan Lam .... 2'02" pg. 216
\# 30 *V'sham'ru/Keep the Sabbath* sung by Philip Goldstein. 5'27" pg. 218
\# 31 *Circles* sung by Patti Linsky .... 2'04" pg. 220
\# 32 *My Dear and Treasured Child* sung by Patti Linsky ...... 4'05" pg. 223
\# 33 *Acharei Moti* sung by Faith Steinsnyder .... 2'38" pg. 226

Chapter 15- Afterward
\# 34 *23rd Psalm* sung by Faith Steinsnyder .... 3'00" pg. 242

•

Introduction

> The Torah in our possession today should not be taken literally (that all the letters of the Torah are the exact ones given to Moses). Rather, the Torah from which we learn and live, contains the intent and purpose of the Torah given to Moses
>
> *—Maimonides in his commentary on Mishnah (Sanhedrin 10:1)*

The underlying reason for writing *Jewish Music As Midrash* reaffirms itself each time I sit down to compose a new Jewish musical setting, whether it is culled from a portion of the liturgy, a sermon in song derived from texts found in the *Tanach* (Torah, Prophets, and Writings), a commemorative work for a life cycle event, or an educational work that illuminates the wisdom of our ancestors. Each time that I study a text and then stare at the stark blankness of the music paper, (or, these days, a computer screen) which confronts me with its urgent latency, I ask myself the same ten questions:

1. What is the intent and purpose that attracts me to this subject?

2. Is it an emotional or intellectual pull or both?

3. What does it mean in the context of the ongoing narrative?

4. What, metaphorically, does it personally mean to me?

5. What do I need to know about its greater literary and non-literary import?

6. Is there more than one interpretation or way of my understanding it?

7. What is the key to making it come alive for me?

8. How can I communicate that chosen meaning through music?

9. Is there a musical *midrash* that I can devise in the process of composition?

10. Ultimately, how do I best communicate this *midrash* to others in the resulting music?

Unlike the romantic notion that music, in its fullest incarnation, is a flash of insight, newly composed music simply does not come to me casually or spontaneously while walking through the woods.

I involve myself in study, methodically immersing myself in both an intellectual and emotional investigation of the literary idea at hand, digesting it until I conceive of the correctness of an ancillary emotional, musical truth.

T.S. Eliot aptly described this process when he wrote:

> We shall not cease from exploration and the end of all our exploring will be to arrive where we started and know the place for the first time.

•

It is only after this study process and absorption of the text that a clear delineation of my personal relationship with it on several levels is defined and refined, until music of any consequence reveals itself to accompany the idea as my personal, supportive, musical *midrash*.

I suspect this is not always the working procedure of other composers or songwriters. Often, instant user friendliness of the melody precludes a deeper search for interpretive elements in it and other parameters that can be employed to enrich the music's function as *midrash*. In defense of beginning composers in the genre, there are no studies to refer to that present the possibility that Jewish music can be a powerful element in forming an effective *midrash*. There have been many books on rabbinic, literary *midrash* but none concentrating on an exploration of the other side of the brain; that is, the *midrashic* functions of music (and art) in Jewish life.

This book is not intended as a comprehensive, historical survey of Jewish musical interpretations or as a musical validation of rabbinic *midrashic* techniques; it is my own personal way of thinking and working as a Jewish sacred music composer and teacher. Here, I attempt to communicate my philosophy and working method to you so that, in addition to understanding Torah through rabbinic, literary *midrashic* commentary, you will also develop the ability to glean an artistic *midrashic* enrichment from musical settings of scripture, liturgy, life-cycle, and wisdom texts. I'm confident that this approach not only works with musical materials, but will also help you more fully appreciate the midrashic potency of the visual arts, dance, and theatre as well.

It is not enough that an artist is born Jewish or gives a Jewish name to a work of art. Jewish art should be made up of much more than these surface attributes. All Jewish music is not equally good. Criteria are needed to discern the difference between lesser and more considered works.

•

These are the four qualities that I use to distinguish a work of significant Jewish art and music:

1. Cognizance of simultaneous time. The work, in some identifiable way, must knowledgeably and simultaneously reflect previous Jewish culture and/or learning, a compelling presence reflecting an aspect of living today, and by the inclusion of creative elements, project the genre into the future, by breaking new interpretive ground or proposing unexplored alternatives in our understanding. Musical settings that are deficient in any one tense are less good than settings that are mindful of these three concurrent potentialities.

2. The work must offer an artistic *midrash* or subjective interpretation of the materials being investigated. If the sole reason for a musical setting is merely to provide a catchy tune, or facilitate memorization of the text, the setting has not realized all that it can add to the larger construct. It is minimal and keeps us on an elementary level of appreciation that impedes a more mature understanding.

3. The work must elevate one's thinking, spirit, and emotive life. I believe as the great British statesman Benjamin Disraeli did that we must

> *Nurture our mind with great thoughts. To believe in the heroic makes heroes.*

The great intellectual battle today is fought in opposition to those who diminish great ideas by trivializing them through quick expediency, lowest common denominator thinking, false economic limitations in shoddy production, and failure to provide an environment both in time and space conducive to understanding the idea's maximum potential impact upon an elevated life. Those who have been appropriately touched by great ideas, presented in the best possible way, know how life transforming and valuable they are.

For those who argue that Jewish music must be always sung by the congregation and never listened to, that it must only be participatory and not presentational, this book responds by suggesting that just as we benefit by listening to a great sermon or *drash* from a learned rabbi, so active listening and understanding of *midrashic* music is equally beneficial and can be quite participatory in bringing the text and its musical setting to an elevated presence in our lives.

The purpose of worship is much more than momentary ecstasy. Victor Frankl in *Man's Search for Meaning* suggests:

> "What man actually needs is not a tensionless state but rather the striving and struggling for some goal worthy of him. What he needs is not the discharge of tension at any cost, but the call of a potential meaning waiting to be fulfilled by him."

4. The artistic work must access the emotive side of the brain, creating a *havdalah*, a separation between the sacred and the mundane.

As a child, I was taught the antithesis of this method at a Yeshiva in Brooklyn, New York. There for the first eight years of my Jewish schooling in the traditional style of the *chayder* (Eastern European religious school), more unfulfilling questions were raised than satisfactory answers provided. The style then, completely "left-brained," was to read, linearly translate, and somehow understand. The pedagogy was completely devoid of affective personality, appropriate learning modality, and personal investigation. Mercifully, one hour each week during my final two years in the seventh and eighth grades, we were given *makeilah* (choir) and my "right brain" saw a bit of sunlight and gasped in the oxygen of the music's spirit. As I have come to understand, the Yeshiva's educational value in my life has been to create, through the void that it created, a negative space, a need for developing a personal alternative method of creative exploration in Jewish life that has stayed with me to this very day over fifty years later. It colors my life and faithfully informs every facet of my spirituality.

Ironically, as much thought as I put into creating an identifiable *midrash* in my musical settings, I suspect that there are still listeners who don't receive the full import, get too little of it, or most unfortunately, are not tuned in at all. I've come to appreciate the truth that for many non-musicians it is hard enough to understand all the ramifications of a text's meanings on a literary level, much less deal with the added density of a musical overlay. Nevertheless, I feel that my mission as a composer of, among other genres, musical settings for Jewish texts would not be complete if I didn't try to help the listener understand the musical *how*—the compositional process, that leads to the *what*—those compositional decisions, that go into creating *midrashic* Jewish music.

As I speak to groups around the world about this subject, the underlying question is always "What makes it Jewish Music?" For many in these audiences, it is the first time that they have even thought about the question and considered how it influences all the music that defines their worship, *simchot* (celebrations), *tzurot* (griefs), life-cycle commemorations, wisdom texts, and, ultimately, their very cultural identity within the larger community and Jewish spectrum of life.

Maimonides (Rambam), the 12th-century Jewish scholar and physician, created an eight-step hierarchy of awareness on the giving of *tzedakah* (virtuous charity) to the poor. The lowest rung begins from the faintest awareness of the *mitzvah* (commandment), by donating begrudgingly, to the highest, ultimate ideal—enabling self-reliance and esteem through teaching a skill or providing employment. I have the notion that the average listener of Jewish music climbs a similar ladder from the faintest awareness of a musical setting to the ideal – a demand for the highest musical expressions founded on an insightful appreciation of the organic relationship between the words and their musical setting. So, with a nod to Rambam's ladder, here is:

Isaacson's Ladder of Musical Awareness:

Rung 1 - "Was there music?"

Rung 2 - "Who listens to music? I don't play an instrument or sing."

Rung 3 - "I don't know that tune."

Rung 4 - "I know that tune."

Rung 5 - "Nice tune."

Rung 6 - "It's always been around; it's traditional."

Rung 7 -   "Is it new. Who composed that tune?"

Rung 8 -   "Oh, it's more than a tune; it's a composition."

Rung 9 -   "Does it have something to do with the words?"

Rung 10 -   "Oh, there is a connection!"

Rung 11 -   "Now I understand the words' meaning more deeply as a result of understanding their relationship to the music."

Rung 12 -   "The text and the musical setting belong together as an entity."

Rung 13 –   "I understand the musical *midrash*."

Where do you think you are on this ladder?

•

It is a long ascent from ignorance to filling the gaps of specific information and knowledge, through awareness, to understanding; but the effort makes all the difference in the world. Sometimes, I feel that too many people are leading spiritual lives like inhabitants of an island situated atop a huge diamond mine, but are oblivious to the treasure buried beneath them. Rather than digging a bit deeper to unearth their riches, they increasingly settle for superficiality; musically ornamenting themselves in too easily acquired shiny trinkets that are, ultimately, little more than transparent glass. This book, *Jewish Music as Midrash,* is offered to help remedy these missed opportunities by sharing with the reader a method of reaching new intellectual, emotional, and spiritual heights by digging more deeply. Once this is understood and mastered, it will enhance the quality of our Jewish music listening experiences and the overall appreciation of religion as well.

This book is meant for lovers of Jewish music who suspect that, in contrast to the banality of the present times, music for spiritual connection should contain and be more than the endless, frenetic, repetition of mispronounced Hebrew words sung to catchy, but stylistically inappropriate tunes.

Jewish Music as Midrash suggests an active listening approach to Jewish music (or to any music for that matter). This skill will help the listener climb the ladder of awareness to access an alternate *midrashic* relationship between a text and its musical setting. It is a relationship that gains emotional insight by adapting and "re-booting" the once solely literary idea of *midrash* with unspoken, but powerful, emotional musical elements.

As the listener (reader) becomes acquainted with how this composer gains insight into Judaism through musical investigation and invention, the reader's own personal mode of accessing the unwritten truths of these great ideas may also become more clearly revealed.

One need not be Jewish nor a musician to benefit from *Jewish Music as Midrash*. It is assumed that the intelligent reader, like most, only has a casual acquaintance with musical terms and practices. Not to be concerned; all these will be explained. In fact, even before its *midrashic* application, this book, like Aaron Copland's wonderful book *What to Listen for in Music*, begins with the art of listening by listing and explaining, in a new way, the identifying traits of music. All Hebrew terms will also be translated into English.

Jewish Music as Midrash is not a dissertation; there are no footnotes. While I have tried to be focused with attributions, the language and presentation of this book are not meant for scholars, but for the average listener who may or may not have some acquaintance with Jewish music. Most importantly, it is meant as a personal expression. I do not presume to represent every composer's processes nor offer a definitive text on either the world of Jewish music or rabbinic *midrash*. All the musical examples are my own.

Music requires the presence of an active listener to be music. Otherwise, it is merely energy. If a tree falls in the forest and no one is there to see or hear it, has it sung its life's song before the fall? In the penta-relationship of Jewish music (music, text, composer, performer, and listener) an informed listening attention is essential to the validity, success, and the very existence of music's creative and communicative efforts and ultimately the elevated understanding of the text. By referring to the examples of the music on the companion CDs, the reader will not only get a practical opportunity to consider the process that I use, but also to listen to music that is the result of it.

In the final analysis, it is always the music that speaks most directly. The questions we consider here are: "Are we too busy singing it to think about it? And are we actively listening to it, or are we merely hearing it?"

•

Chapter 1
Mastering the Challenges of Listening

All speech, written or spoken, is a dead language, until it finds a willing and prepared listener.
—*Robert Louis Stevenson*

One evening, as I often do as a composer and music educator, I presented a recorded work of American Jewish music to a group of highly educated professional people. They were literate in Hebrew and Jewish texts and were dynamically interested affiliated Jews. This distinguished professional gathering included doctors, lawyers, engineers, educators, and even a few visual artists.

The composition that I offered was a colleague's musical *midrash* in the form of a setting of a poem found in a *siddur* (prayer book). It was scored for solo soprano voice and women's chorus accompanied by piano, cello, and flute. The duration of the musical work was thirteen minutes.

Before I played it, I read the poem that served as its text and briefly discussed its meaning, context, and the backgrounds of both the author and the composer. I suggested images that each person might call up as they listened and some musical metaphors that they would hear. In other words, I prepared the group for the thirteen minute listening experience.

As I customarily do after pushing the play button on the CD player, I sat back and intently watched the group's reaction to the piece. As a conductor and a music producer, I've also learned that one can discern the strengths and impact of a piece of music by observing the audience's movements and sounds during its performance.

All was fine for the first few minutes. At about six minutes into the listening experience there was some subtle shuffling of bodies in the seats. I label this activity ZDS – *Zitzfleisch Deficiency Syndrome.* The lack of *zitzfleisch* (literally in Yiddish "the flesh you sit on") is the restlessness of body and/or spirit that causes people to squirm or shuffle in their seats. The next time you go to a concert look for it among the audience, and you will be both amused and informed.

If you can remember where the music was at that point, you will undoubtedly learn something as well about the music's communicative powers and weaknesses.

At about nine minutes, the ZDS was coupled with intermittent throat clearing and coughing; sure signs that, though it was neither a late hour nor flu season, the audience was beginning to experience significant obstacles in "breathing in" the music's aural journey. At eleven minutes, there were one or two stifled yawns, and one person actually excused herself from the room. At the conclusion of the thirteen-minute work, all appreciatively and (no doubt) gratefully applauded.

While this entire group heard the music only a handful actually listened to the music. Hearing and listening, as composer Aaron Copland observed in his book *What To Listen For In Music,* are quite different phenomena. Hearing is the involuntary, passive, automatic, physical reception of sounds, while listening occurs on a much higher level and is the voluntary, active, selective, processing of this aural data into intellectually and emotionally meaningful stimuli. We hear millions of sounds each day, but we only listen to a very few.

Why was it so difficult for some members of this highly intelligent group to concentrate on the music's unfolding message? It was only thirteen minutes long. What obstacles impeded their minds and hearts from connecting with the music and precluded an optimally successful listening experience? Can you imagine what must take place during a one-hour Mahler symphony or, heaven forbid, a full evening of a Wagnerian opera?

There are several reasons for the rapid onset of ZDS in epidemic proportions in contemporary life. Some are environmental and collective, while others are due to our own individual, personal level of education and training.

Environmentally, one reason may be summarized as coping with the raw quantity and quality of sounds, in the absence of adequate processing time. Consider the quantity of sounds that we hear each day. If we live in an urban community, as most of us do, from the minute we wake up to the alarm clock, shower, hair dryer, electric toothbrush, coffee maker, microwave, and the trash removal trucks outside, to the ubiquitous TV and radio with their plethora of news bulletins, commercials, and sound bytes, to the traffic and work noises, to the omnipresent mindless elevator and call-waiting music, to the computer prompts, to our colleague's and customer's questions and answers, to dozens of phone calls (and recorded messages), to a wealth of conversations, our days are filled with sound and very little silence.

If we were to assign equal importance to each sound that we hear and actually listen in detail, we'd have very little or no time for any consequential activity. For our own efficiency (and, indeed, sanity) we have taught ourselves to hear but not to listen. Not only don't we listen, but because of the bulk volume of sound, our individual reaction time (deciding not to listen) becomes shorter and shorter. We have trained ourselves to assess the quality and import of each sound all the more superficially, giving it an instant discount rating.

Martin Buber valued quiet moments as a remedy for this frenzy; *"Solitude is the place of purification,"* he noted. Nevertheless, we have become expedient automatons, taking aural shortcuts, which prevent the possibilities of deeper musical meaning from enriching our lives.

Our young, especially, demand music with an incessant drum beat that shouts out to us (even at trendy worship services): "It's ok to hear me but don't give me any real thought!"

It wasn't always so. Before TV and radio, even at the inception of the Industrial Age there were far less sounds in the world bombarding us and demanding our full attention. We actually sought to involve ourselves in more music of longer forms.

In Beethoven's lifetime (1770-1827), during the late Classical Period through the early Romantic Period (1820-1850), the actual time span of an evening's concert was more than two times longer than the concerts presented today. Fewer of our ancestors had wristwatches or were clock-watchers.

On the first half there might be an overture, piano concerti and a symphony, then a break for dinner and/or liquid refreshment, and then an equally long second half to the evening. Wagner could conceive of his *Ring* cycle because audiences were capable of inputting and processing it; they knew how and were accustomed to sitting still and listening to music over an extended period of time. They also ascribed an importance to it because, outside the concert hall, they did not have access to recorded performances. The concert experience was a musically unique phenomenon, both in its separation and elevation from everyday life.

These historical and cultural occurrences dramatically color our value system. When we are given the time and opportunity to consider sounds, we can assign hierarchical importance to what we value (and even treasure). What we cannot readily assess, we quickly devalue. It takes extended periods of silence and introspection to make these meanings. Regretfully, too few of us allow these moments of silent processing to be scheduled into our over-programmed everyday existences (and worship).

While our collective environment no doubt hampers our listening process, our personal level of music education and listening experience (or lack thereof) puts the final nail in the coffin.

When Thomas Jefferson rested his pen, as he pondered the features of the Declaration of American Independence that he was assigned to author, he would customarily pick up his violin and play to clear his mind and open his heart. Was he a virtuoso? Perhaps not, but he considered himself an educated man in an enlightened civilized world. Playing a musical instrument was representative of that education. Benjamin Franklin actually composed string quartets.

There was a time at the beginning of the 20th century when every respectable middle-class home had a piano in the parlor. This was hardly due to a great mass wealth of keyboard prodigies in America, but simply because music making (even on the most modest level)—not simply passive music hearing on an iPod—was considered by many humanists to be basic educational literacy like reading, writing and arithmetic.

During my own formative years in the nineteen-fifties and sixties, growing up in Brooklyn, New York, public school education always included both choral and instrumental music instruction. Today, in spite of educational enrichment lotteries and seductive political promises, it is rare to find a quality music instructional program in a public school.

In Santa Monica, California, there is a convenience store that slyly pipes classical music out in front of its entrance to dissuade teens from congregating there.

Regrettably, because of today's lack of music education in our schools, our inability to listen patiently and intelligently to meaningful music will continue to be a trend well into the next generation.

In synagogue music, by the "trickle-down" theory, this lack of musical knowledge will proliferate the demand for less meaningful Jewish music from songwriters instead of composers, and for performances by song leaders instead of cantors.

Music is a language with grammar and syntax, like English or Hebrew. But before we can understand what these ordered sounds are saying to us, we must be conversant in its "sentence structure." Today, most of us have unlimited access on our computers and iPods to downloadable music in amounts inconceivable just a few years ago. Yet, we are basically illiterate in the language of music and its attendant listening skills. While we hear more music each day than ever before in the history of our species, we actively listen to far less.

My effectiveness as author of *Jewish Music as Midrash* is directly dependent upon your acquired, skillful ability to ingest and consider the music that I offer as recorded examples on the companion CDs, and to understand something about its language and syntax, and how to listen actively to it.

As the Jewish Spanish philosopher and poet Solomon Ibn Gabirol suggested, *"The beginning of wisdom is to desire it."* So, towards achieving this goal, here are five brief recommendations that will help you hurdle the initial obstacles of active listening and perceiving music far more deeply and significantly than you may currently do.

•

1.   Before listening to any music, listen to the silence that precedes it.

We buy a new CD of music. We want to get the most out of it. Before we put it on and really listen, let's treat ourselves to a few moments of silence, clearing our mind of other issues and allowing ourselves the serenity of one or two deep, cleansing breaths to wash away anxieties, mad calculations, and frenzied scheduling.

In this way we create a space where the music can enter less challenged or encumbered by other assertive considerations.

Perhaps, we might want to meditate as we concentrate on our breathing, reflecting on the approaching experience and how it will enable us to become refreshed, elevated, and apart from the banalities that surround us. We might visualize ourselves alone on a non-threatening island. We are safe and in need of nothing. We allow ourselves to relax in that nothingness for a few moments, breathing fully and deeply. We then, quietly open the CD booklet and begin reading, preparing for the music to which we will listen. This relinquishing of past preoccupations and the anxieties of the future is called "being in the moment" or "being present."

This same approach can be utilized in a concert hall with live music. Arrive at the hall a few minutes earlier than usual. Take off your coat, get comfortable in your seat, and do not immediately open your program to read it. Instead, close your eyes, dismiss the stresses of traffic that brought you to the concert hall, the hassle of obtaining tickets, and admission, and again, breathing deeply and steadily, clearing your mind of past concerns, reflect on an empty, quiet space that is warm and inviting. No one demands anything of you, and you are in full control of the solitude. Give yourself the gift of this quiet preparation. It will make all the difference. Then, and only then, begin to read the program and intellectually prepare yourself for the music that you are about to hear.

The same opportunity exists when we go to a house of worship. Nachmanides, the medieval Talmudic scholar, wrote in 1268, *"When you pray, remove from your heart all worldly concerns."*

How is this achieved? Before opening the prayer book and jumping in to access the spiritual experience, we should punctuate the past urgencies. Rest our eyes and ears, not speaking nor looking around, breathing deeply, giving ourselves license to enter a new space that is unencumbered and willing to accept the quiet voice of godliness. In other words, use silence to cleanse the spirit as a chef uses sorbet between courses to cleanse the palate. In quieting the past we enable the fullness of the present and begin to conceive of future eternity.

Author Michael Halperin addresses this holiness of preparation when he writes:

> Pray before the praying begins,
> When the quiet reigns across the softening sky,
> When light enters and searches out
> Secrets I did not know I kept.
> Pray before the prayer begins,
> Not filled with hallelujahs and amens,
> Not sated with familiar vows,
> Nor clotted with the fat of prose.
> Spare signs will do—
> Smiles.
> Hands.
> Touch.
> Texture.
> The prayer before the prayer begins.

Listening to a CD, attending a concert, or worshipping, in all three cases we separate the present special moment from the cluttered past. Preparation and separation are valued concepts in Judaism. When I composed my *Havdalah Suite* (separation from the Sabbath), I began with a *nigun* (a wordless melody) as a preparatory meditation for the experience of ending the Sabbath. Its function was solely to give us time to take a breath and make available that quiet space where content could be thoughtfully and sensitively accepted and appreciated, without distracting interference. Preparation is essential in dividing time and content and enabling us to separate ourselves, even momentarily, from the weight and pressure of the past.

Yehuda Al-Charizi, the 12th century Spanish poet and translator, wrote in his *Sefer Tahkemoni*, "*When is prayer heard? When the soul is subdued?*" The separation and preparation of silence affords the listener a moment of cleansing, enabling listening to what follows to be hallowed and elevated. Greater attention is paid to the music.

Play recorded example #1 on the companion CD – *Nigun for Sabbath's Farewell* sung by Cantor Roslyn Barak. As you listen, breathe deeply and get to know it as a preparatory meditation.

•

2. Create a mental template of the musical structure you are about to hear.

To appreciate this recommendation, we must understand the difference between seeing visual art and listening to aural art (music). When we look at a painting, the structural entirety is there before us. After observing the gestalt, we might focus in on this aspect of the structural detail or that aesthetic characteristic, always referring back to the structural entirety to see how each facet contributes to the overall impact.

This is not possible with music. While visual art is structured in space, music is structured in time. At any given second we only are hearing a fragment of a sound. Our memories then recall that sound and attach it to the next audible sound, creating a larger construct that we might call a melody or a rhythm. But, acoustically, all we are hearing at any given moment is a speck of a sound's fragment.

The acuity of our memory is the major strength in listening to music. If we can remember the sounds from the more distant past and connect them with the sound that we are hearing at the moment, then we have a chance to compare and contrast the two and understand their structural relationship with each other, where they might proceed to, and the sum total that we call music.

Why is listening to a rock song so much easier? Because this form doesn't demand that we remember much. Instead, it constantly repeats most elements of itself so that the incessant repetition does the work for us. If we take into account the number of times the drumbeat repeats, the melody repeats, the lyric repeats, and the rhythm and harmony repeat, a three to five minute structural experience only demands fifteen to thirty seconds of our attentive intelligence. Of course, it will be understood more easily.

For the thinking listener, the trick to remembering sounds and understanding their relationships with each other is to use a mental template as a guide. A template is a form where content can be filled into a receiving structure.

When we go to a baseball game, few of us can remember by heart the details of what happened during the nine or more innings. We use the score sheet in the game program to jot down each play and position, thereby following the action (structure) of the game and recalling it in its entirety upon demand.

When we play golf, we use a scorecard to remember our strokes on each hole and recall the dynamics (structure) of the entire eighteen-hole encounter. We even make grocery lists to guide our trip (structure) through the aisles in obtaining the groceries that we need to be economically effective consumers. Picturing what might occur and then what actually has occurred helps us remember the experience.

It is the same with listening to music. As music is a journey through time, we need a way to recall aspects of it to remember its whole idea (structure). Making a mental outline, scorecard, or template takes an aural abstraction and converts it, by this visual aid, into a workable reality.

We are so much more experienced visually than we are aurally. When you visit an affluent home you may see highly sophisticated abstract art on the walls, but the music being played on the state-of-the-art sound system is hardly abstract at all. It is usually the same or similar representational sounds that were heard, formerly, in childhood. We accept visual abstractions much more readily than we can assimilate (and remember) musical abstractions.

How do we make a musical template before we even listen to one note of music?

The answer is that we learn as much as we can about the structure of the piece from the program notes, CD booklet notes, *siddur*, and preparatory literature with similarities that create a general mental outline encouraging expectations. What might we hear? Will it sound as expected? In other words, we create a template that will be filled with fully or less gratified sound expectations.

When you train your mind to create these templates, it opens up to receiving sound in a much more user-friendly way.

Here's an illustration in sound. Example #2 on the companion CD: **Yism'chu (They Will Rejoice)** from my Sabbath service *Nishmat Chayim (The Breath of Life)*.

Play recorded example #2 **Yism'chu,** sung by Cantor Faith Steinsnyder, accompanied by women's chorus, woodwind quintet (flute, oboe, clarinet, French horn, and bassoon), and organ.

Here is the template of the structure:

INTRODUCTION by the Woodwind Quintet

SECTION A - cantor sings refrain / chorus repeats

SECTION B – cantor sings first verse / chorus repeats

SECTION A - cantor sings refrain / chorus repeat

SECTION C – cantor sings bridge (middle) / chorus repeats

SECTION A - cantor sings refrain / chorus repeats

SECTION B – cantor sings third verse / chorus repeats

SECTION A - chorus sings refrain / cantor repeats

CODA (ending "tail" also known as an "outro") sung by the entire ensemble

Or in shorthand, the template may be summarized as:

Intro   ABA   C   ABA   Coda

This template is the same kind a conductor makes in his mind to memorize the score and remember when to cue the singers and instruments. In this case, it contains one minute and forty-three seconds of musical content.

Listen to this short piece again, following the template.

Isn't it easier now to expect certain musical sections? When we expect a musical event, we are actively listening. Even if we have not ever heard the piece before, by referring to our mental template and expecting the events on the template, we will be actively listening for the first time and remembering more of what we hear. Our ZDS will be less, and we will not yawn so quickly.

Try making a template of your favorite song in the same way and notice how the repetitions build an overt structure with expectations.

3. Once the template is made, fill in greater details while you listen.

Using example two on the companion CD once again, notice how:

a. The cantor sings for eight beats and the chorus repeats for eight beats.

b. The woodwinds and organ vary the accompaniment in each new section.

c. The text changes in each new section. What does the text mean? How is the woodwind instrumentation illuminating the meaning?

Yism'chu — "They Will Rejoice"

Those who keep the Sabbath and call it a delight shall rejoice in Your deliverance. All who hallow the seventh day shall be gladdened by Your goodness. This day is Israel's festival of the spirit, sanctified and blessed by You, the most precious of days, a symbol of the joy of creation.

This aural process is analogous to seeing the totality of a painting and then going off to explore its different aspects, always referring back to the larger structure to make the meaning even more clear.

Making a template and identifying the structural sections of it doesn't have to be as clinical as I have suggested. We might just say in our minds that the cantor and choir trade off the melody accompanied by the winds. As long as expectations are created, we will actively listen for them.

Of course, the more details we listen for, the more rewarding it is to hear and appreciate the performance art that went into gratifying our expectations. We will remember more fully the meaning that the composer puts into the music. Sometimes we achieve this through repeated hearings, and sometimes we achieve this, initially, by developing the sophistication and depth of our active listening through multiple former experiences of a similar nature.

4. Bring life experience of comparisons to each template.

What makes an artistic experience better or fuller than another? As soon as we use the word "than" we are comparing experiences.

This is how meanings are made. A baby tastes strained pears and understands that it is different than the strained bananas she tasted before. Only when expectations are created, and differences and similarities are understood and developed, can tastes be identified and preferences be made.

To continue the analogy: if the baby had trouble taking in the foods, she would have a harder time tasting and appreciating the menu before her, and deciding what she liked best.

In other words, before we can truly like or dislike, appreciate or discount, treasure or disregard anything in our lives, we, in all fairness, must learn how to most effectively "take it in," so that we can compare it with our previous experiences and expectations.

While a painting is static and set as a single object, music can have several different live or recorded interpretive performances (gratified or frustrated expectations). Once we have a filled template we can then make meanings and choose our favorite version of the music. So, before listening, we retrieve data files from our memory banks and ask ourselves:

1. What other similar musical experiences can I use to access this new experience?

2. What other version of *Yism'chu* do I know?

   a. Who performed it?

   b. How was it performed?

3. Have I heard a cantor and choir sing together before?

   a. During what other musical occasions have I heard this?

   b. Under what performing circumstances?

   c. What text were they performing?

   d. Was it the same text or a different one?

4. Have I heard a woodwind quintet play before?

   a. What music was it playing?

   b. Was it played skillfully?

   c. Did I like or dislike it?

It goes without saying that the more listening experiences we have the more we can remember similarities and differences and make meanings more profoundly through educated comparison. Can you now appreciate that, while I presented a single recorded musical performance to one room of people, several different levels of memory received the music making it several very different artistic experiences? This is the fascinating aspect of music. It exists in time and memory and no two memories are the same.

5. Ask yourself: "What was the transformational power of this musical experience?"

There is music that is so much like other music that we have already heard that there are no revelations in it for us. We hear it, discount it, or listen superficially, and evaluate it as an indistinguishable repetition of a former experience. How much of this do we encounter each day both outside and within the synagogue? Far too much!

Then there is the music that's different. It addresses an issue in an unexpected way. Just as a striking visual piece opens our eyes, an originally conceived piece of music opens our ears. It informs us of greater possibilities and offers us a wider spectrum of colors and ideas. We are transformed, becoming "new" beings, more elevated, more insightful, more close to our Godliness and ideal image of a more perfectly varied world of revelations. This transformational moment is what we all aspire to and hope for in our lives.

Just as we prepared in silence before listening to a piece of music, so, at the conclusion of a listening let us not leave it so quickly. Consider and savor it for a moment, giving our minds a chance to input and "process" its impact by asking ourselves:

1. Did this moment transform me? How?

2. How do I understand anew?

3. How do I feel anew?

4. How do I redefine my world now?

5. How can I use this transformation and the goodness or gratitude that I feel to help others and myself?

You might be thinking to yourself: "I don't have the time to go through this extended thought process every time I hear a piece of music or look at a work of art."

Do not be concerned. The mind and heart work in nanoseconds, and what I have taken pages to lay out only takes a fraction of a moment in a thinking person's real time. This is the wonder of ordered meaning and the elevated position that human beings can enjoy, if we will only allow ourselves access to more profound meaning on a regular basis.

An audience is defined as a group who is actively seeing and listening to a presentation, not merely passively looking at, or absentmindedly hearing it.

The important thing to remember about all this is, that just as we would not go to an art museum and put on blindfolds, so each time we are given the opportunity to receive a gift of music, we must take the "earplugs of indifference" out of our ears and listen consciously, with expectations and interest, in detail. It is the conscious act of paying attention and becoming a vital part of the complete connection between the composer, the composition, the performer, and us.

To master the challenges of listening and receiving more information and enjoyment, develop these five listening procedures:

1. Before listening to any music, listen to the silence preceding it.

2. Create a mental template of the musical structure about to be heard.

3. Once the template is made, fill in greater details while listening and re-listening.

4. Bring life experience of comparisons to each template.

5. In the silence that follows the music ask, "What was the transformative power of this musical experience?" and, "How has it changed me?"

Succinctly put, actively listening to music enables you to really hear it. Once these challenges are mastered, celebrate a transformational experience. You might find yourself less satisfied with non-transformational moments. It is very much like eating a wonderful gourmet meal and being less eager to follow it with a fast food snack.

We are meant to seek out these experiences. They surround us everyday. They are in the sights we see, the music we listen to, the foods we taste, the aromas we smell, and the relationships we nurture. Once these first steps of active listening are mastered, we can then relish the even greater powers of mining and understanding the musical *midrash* inherent in each of these transformative moments.

•

Chapter 2
The Identifying Traits of Music

Writing has laws of perspective, of light and shade just as painting does, or music. If you are born knowing them, fine. If not, learn them. Then rearrange the rules to suit yourself. — *Truman Capote*

The idea of presuming to teach what music is made up of in one chapter is so daunting that I have to pause to consider even bringing up the subject. Music, of course, is a lifetime study that is infinite in its detail and myriad in its possibilities. And yet, at this juncture, if we do not begin to share some useful information, some language and terminology that describe the identifying features of music, I would feel more like Shamai than Hillel. Let me explain.

In the *Babylonian Talmud* in tractate *Shabbat 31a*, there is a famous contrast made between the demeanors of Rabbi Shamai and his disciples (the House of Shamai), who were concerned with the pure essence of ideas and laws, and Rabbi Hillel and his school, who were more pragmatic. These two classic debaters argue (to our great benefit) the finer points of the oral law *(Mishneh)*, complementing the written law that is the Torah. While Shamai's students may have been more legally skillful, they lacked the "popular touch" that the House of Hillel offered. This distinction is illustrated in a story of a rascal who made a bet of four hundred zuzim that he could make Rabbi Hillel lose his temper. After a round of silly questions, all of which Hillel thoughtfully and patiently answered, the story continues:

> On another occasion a certain heathen came before Shamai and said to him, "Make me a proselyte [a religious believer], on condition that you teach me the whole Torah while I stand on one foot."
>
> Thereupon he [Shamai] repulsed him with a builder's cubit [a ruler] that was in his hand.
>
> When the heathen went before Hillel, he said to him, "What is hateful to you, do not to your neighbor: that is the whole Torah; the rest is the commentary thereof. Go and learn it."

I wish I could describe music while "standing on one foot" as elegantly and popularly as Hillel encapsulated the Torah, but to begin to relate music to midrash we must have some musical terminology that will help us recognize the building blocks. Then, like Hillel, I, too, will advise you to take the initiative and "go and learn" more by listening and studying.

First of all, music (even improvisation) is organized sound. Each musical sound has a beginning (attack), middle (duration), and an end (decay). Like language, it expresses itself in basic units of ideas (motifs) that combine together to create larger forms and structures (phrases, periods, sections, and movements). There are also seven other identifying features that will help us think and talk about the music we listen to more clearly.

In the last chapter, on the challenges of listening, it was observed that our visual sophistication is far greater than our aural skills. This is because music lives in memory, rather than the way visual art presents its totality all at once. With musical memory, to stay on track, we, as capable sound trackers, must know where we've been, where we are, and where we are going.

Consequently, if our visual analytic skills are more developed at this point than our aural acuity, using visual, theatrical analogies when explaining these seven identifying musical sound characteristics will clarify and facilitate understanding of them. In fact,

I'll employ a theatrical cast of stage players to make my points more dramatically.

1. The first character(istic) is melodic **pitch,** or **tone. Pitch** can be compared to the words in the script used in a dramatic play. Each word (melodic note) relates to another (closer or farther melodic intervals) creating larger and more developed images (motifs, scales, arpeggios). If certain words have greater intensity (closer, more dissonant intervals), then the dramatic moment becomes greater. If the words are soothing (intervals more spread out, and less dissonant), other emotions, like romance and humor might be explored.

Like words in a sentence, these extended ideas (melodic phrases) create expectancies. If an actor says, "You must pay the rent," then we would expect the actress to answer, "But I can't pay the rent." If this is what we hear, it is an expected resolution (or full cadence). If it is not what we hear, it may be a thought that is continuing on (a half cadence). "What, you say you can't pay the rent?" Or, it might take a deceptive cadence, "Then marry me, my love, and I'll pay the rent!" The central issue is that melodies, like verbal sentences, create expectancies that our ears hear and our minds anticipate. This active anticipation is what keeps us interested in the progress of the story (the melodic journey). As expectancy is gratified we input and use it as substantiating material to understand the next expectancy.

As listeners, while we are enjoying a melody unfold we are also asking, "Where is this going – here or there?" This curious anticipation keeps us attentive to the melodic progress and the eventual relationships that our melody will encounter with other musical characters. This fascination with the melody's direction enables us to listen more actively and wisely. While there are examples of percussion music that is all rhythm and no pitch, whenever we speak of a melody or a tune, we are also referring to the intervallic relationship of their pitches or tones with each other.

2. The second character(istic) is **Rhythm.** Using silence, the opposite aspect of sound, we can break up sections of melodies to create regular and irregular patterns. If an actor is talking fast and furiously, and then stops to give another character a tacit look or silently fume, and then resumes talking again, that actor's speech (melody) would be said to have a definite rhythm. Silence enables us to hear sound. If every sound was continuous we could not understand it because it would have no beginning or end. It would be one long hum. Silence between sounds defines the boundaries of the sound itself.

Just as in a conversation between two impassioned actors, the less silence there is in between the words the more animated or heated the dialogue becomes.

Because we have less time to use the interim silence in listening and considering the words, we, too, become more anxious and excited. This is why faster rhythms stimulate us, while slower rhythms calm us down.

As listeners, our awareness of the use of silence in melodies (rhythmic articulation) helps us make sense of the sound. The faster frequency of silence between sounds creates tension and propels our interest in the musical idea's forward thrust (exposition and development).

3. The third character(istic) is **Harmony.** Harmony may be understood as parallel, multiple speeches (melodies) recited by

two or more actors simultaneously (or in counterpoint). If each speech (melody) works well on its own, it contributes to a more intense dramatic super effect when it combines with the other speeches. One actor might speak faster while another slower, creating a harmonic rhythm.

One might use calming words (consonant melodic intervals), while another might use more intense inflammatory language (dissonant melodic intervals). One might speak louder than the other, giving importance and singular emphasis.

Together, we understand not only each individual speech but also the super-relationship one speech has, simultaneously, with another. Here, the whole is greater than the sum of its parts.

Sometimes historians (harmonic theorists) go back to study plays (compositions) and see recurring stock relationships (harmonic analysis) in the simultaneous speeches. These are used so frequently that they become idiomatic (fundamental harmony). Like a Commedia Dell'arte ensemble, they will then offer these "stock characters" (chord symbols) as a way of expediting the process of character development. The point is that these harmonies first started out in life as fresh expressions, created as relationships between two, three, or more melodies, and worked so well that they were used over and over again to form a common, mutual harmonic language accompanied by a shorthand called chords. A chord is vertical shorthand, but the best harmony is most frequently composed horizontally or linearly as the relationship of individual melodies or lines.

As listeners, our opportunity will not only be to discern one melody, but also two or more melodies in counterpoint, and become attuned to listening to the relationship (the harmony) between them. Harmony need not be pretty in a consonant way. It might be jagged, or even ugly. But, no matter what the dramatic attitude, the harmony helps us understand each melody and the relationships they simultaneously share with other melodies.

4. The fourth character(istic) is **Dynamics.** In 1525, the Northern German artist Albrecht Dürer began experimenting with vanishing points as a way of creating a third dimension of depth in two dimensional paintings. In 1660 the use of raked stages in French drama became a theatrical convention. Then in 1750 (last, of course), musical dynamics were included in scores and became standardized. What do vanishing points, raked stages, and musical dynamics have in common?

Albrecht Dürer, (1471-1528) the great etcher and painter from Nuremberg, authored a *Painter's Manual* in 1525 that described single and multiple vanishing points to create the illusion of depth and perspective in visual art. This began a humanistic trend that understood the world geometrically and empowered humankind to fear the world less and go on to explore it boldly.

Have you ever read the script of a play that had the stage direction, "character moves downstage," or the admonition from a director not to "upstage the other actor"? Upstage and downstage directions come from the Renaissance period when dirt stages were actually raked so that it was higher towards the rear of the stage and lower down front. This also allowed stage scenery to give the illusion of depth.

When an actor walked "downstage," he was closer to the audience and could be heard more clearly. It soon became a theatrical convention that important information furthering the plot would be delivered nearer to the audience (downstage), while less important embellishing lines could be spoken farther away (upstage). If all the information were delivered upstage, it might not be heard, and if all the information were spoken downstage, it would lack relief.

So, a balance was soon created between the characters' blocking (stage movement) and the information heard upstage and downstage. If a minor character was out-doing another at an inappropriate moment, the director, for the sake of balance, might scold the actor not to "upstage" the dominant performer. Or, conversely, if the dramatic line needed more emphasis, the director would urge the performer to speak it downstage.

Dynamics in music work the very same way. When we apply the Italian dynamics mezzo piano – (mp - medium soft), piano – (p - soft), pianissimo – (pp - very soft), and pianissisimo – (ppp - softest), we want the audience to consider that melody "upstage" and farther away from us than a melody marked mezzo forte – (mf - medium loud), forte – (f - loud), fortissimo – (ff - louder still), and fortissisimo – (fff, which, in effect, booms in our faces).

Parenthetically, the modern piano's full name is "pianoforte" because, when the keyboard mechanism was changed from the quiet, intimate plucking of a string on a harpsichord to the more overt hitting of the string by a felt hammer, the reconceived instrument became able to create a wider spectrum of both soft and loud sounds.

As listeners, dynamics are important guidelines steering us to the melody that is most informative at the moment. Composers mark a melody forte when they want you to take note if it and they mark a melody piano when they want it to play a subordinating, accompanying role or a dramatically contrasting part. Understanding the function of dynamics creates three-dimensional perspective in music, just as the Renaissance use of perspective and vanishing lines in drawing created depth in the visual arts, and a raked stage provided the illusion of depth in the performing arts.

5. The fifth identifying character(istic) is **Tempo.** From the Latin for time, tempo is how slowly or quickly a musical idea is performed. After establishing the tempo by observing one of the many initial Italian tempo markings (from slowest to fastest) like Lento, Largo, Adagio, Andante, Allegro, Molto Allegro, Vivace, and Presto, we can speed up the tempo (accelerando), moving us into the future more rapidly, or slow down the tempo (ritardando), enabling us to savor the present a bit more.

A conductor's responsibility is not only to cue the entrances and exits of melodic lines, but also to direct and control the loudness and softness (dynamic), and slowness or quickness (tempo) of the performance.

As listeners, we can understand that slower tempi (plural of tempo) are more meditative and brooding than faster tempi, which are more athletic and adventurous. Just as color changes our perception of a melody, so does its tempo as well.

6. The sixth identify trait in music is **Style.** Just as a set designer or costumer uses specific visual guidelines and conventions to suggest a particular time or place, so a composer sets limitations on what sounds will be used and not used in a particular musical style. Understanding the particular sound vocabulary,

or rules of the piece (whatever they are set up to be), and finding the elegance and freedom within those limitations, is the key to appreciating a musical work's stylistic integrity and ultimate creativity. While the inclusion of many styles in one patch quilt is often touted as eclecticism, it really is a rationalization for the absence of a more well-defined, more limited, singular stylistic sense.

For example, it is one thing for the music of a worship service to be stylistically eclectic for the political strategy of pleasing a heterogeneous congregation, and quite another due to a lack of performance skill or the informed discipline to limit the styles that are being incorporated.

7.   The seventh and final character(istic) is **Color** (French: **Timbre** pronounced "tamber"). Just as a costumer outfits an actor in a costume whose color will help him communicate the lightness or heaviness, the vibrancy or drabness, the serious or humorous nature of his role, so the specific solo instrument or group of instruments that perform a specific melody color the attitude and intensity of that melodic line.

There are the four basic sub-groups or sections of instruments in an orchestra. The woodwinds, from highest to lowest, are the piccolo, flute, oboe, English horn, clarinet, bass clarinet, bassoon, and contrabassoon.

The French horn is a connecting instrument sometimes considered a woodwind and sometimes a brass. The brass, from highest to lowest, are the trumpet, French horn, trombone, and the tuba.

The next sub-group or family is the percussion section. This is an interesting burgeoning group that began in the Baroque Period from, basically, tympani, cymbals, and drums to a modern rainbow of instruments today that now include chimes, xylophones, marimbas, glockenspiels, piano, and celesta and exotic drums, shakers, rattles, and cymbals from all around the world, as well as novelty instruments like the saw, wind machine, inverted flower pots, and brake drums.

The most conspicuous orchestral section is the oldest and the largest. The strings, from highest to lowest, are the violin, viola, cello, and bass. Sometimes the harp and piano are also included in this family as vibrating strings also produce their sound. In a modern orchestra there might be as many as fifty or more string players and a combination of fifty brass, woodwind, and percussion players.

Today, in electronic music, these acoustic orchestral instruments are often synthetically emulated and join the nearly infinite number of purely electronic sounds that make up the composer's sound palette.

Color is not just an instrumental domain. Colors can be assigned to voices as well. Singers are often asked to "darken" or "lighten" their sounds. In addition to individual vocal modifications, choruses achieve color gradations by varying the combination of the women's brightness in the sopranos and altos with the darker (one octave lower) sounds of the men's tenor and bass sections.

As listeners, following the assignment of melodies and harmonies in certain sections of the larger ensemble, color helps us stay with the developing idea's odyssey. At the same time, we are also charmed by how the same melody takes on a new, colorful "costume" by being played by different instruments or sung by different voice types.

To recapitulate, the seven identifying traits that all types of music possess:

Pitch

Rhythm

Harmony

Dynamic

Tempo

Style

Timbre

•

Now that we have some terminology to use when thinking and talking about music, how, indeed, do we use it? The first step towards understanding is always observation.

The intelligent listener uses a complete brain, thinking and noticing the intellectual idea while, at the same time, sensing and feeling the emotion. Just as an enthralled, intelligent viewer appreciates a painting by taking notice of the line (melody), the ratio of negative space (silence) surrounding a positive image (sound), which together create a rhythm, the viewer also notes how diverse elements relate to each other (harmony), the perspective and emphasis of elements (dynamics), how relaxed or frenetic the image is (tempo), and the colors (timbre) of each section that blend to create the overall effect. The active listener also "observes" these components as the sound journey unfolds and develops.

You can keep track of these identifying traits like a baseball scorecard, e.g., "In the second section, when the oboe plays the rapid, rhythmic figure, and the flute plays a descending minor melody against it . . ." helps us fill in our mental template's recollection of these melodic, rhythmic, harmonic, dynamic, timbrel, and tempo features, aiding us in remembering where we and the music were, where we and the music are presently, and even perhaps, where we and the music are going.

When recalling musical moments, don't hesitate to scribble in your concert program and use these terms just as you would use "strike, ball, and foul" to remember what a batter did at bat in a particular inning during a baseball game. The more you remember and can recall, the more you have intelligently listened to the music and have actively heard it.

Throughout this chapter we've assigned human traits to musical abstractions. Using this technique of making musical elements come alive, like actors on a stage, helps us "visually" understand these identifying materials more clearly and solve musical issues, which, by their abstract character, might temporarily perplex. This approach helps listeners see and hear more clearly and appreciate the balance of all these traits more knowingly.

A midrashic interpretation of these traits might also include these observations:

Melody – Our life script is most "playable" and "listenable" when there is a melodic balance of consonance and dissonance.

Rhythm – Slowing down and listening complements accelerating and talking.

Harmony—It is the full awareness of two or more sides of a relationship (consonance and dissonance) that define and promote its harmony.

Dynamic – We enable others to be when we are silent or quieter than they are.

Tempo—It is the balance of speed and repose in our lives that enables us to live in simultaneous time frames.

Style – In limitation there is freedom and focus.

Timbre – A colorful life is best achieved by knowing where we fit in the rainbow.

In other words, each characteristic of music holds the potential for commentary. A composer or performer, to infuse philosophy, psychology, and other various overlays of coloration and interpretation upon a Jewish text, event, or artistic articulation of an idea, may use each or all of these parameters (traits).

Well, there you have it in a nutshell, *"al regel achat* —on one foot."

Now, go and listen. Listen to all kinds of music, both vocal and instrumental, in all styles, and identify the traits as you listen. In a short time you will surprise yourself by beginning to hear and identify the multiple traits that every sound possesses. When this occurs, you will have reached a higher level of active listening and will be able to begin accessing the even more fascinating, symbolic world of musical *midrash.*

•

Chapter 3
What Makes Music Jewish?
A Conundrum Wrapped in an Enigma

It is rather the Hebrew spirit that interests me, the complex, ardent, agitated soul that vibrates for me in the Bible. The vigor and ingeniousness of the patriarchs, the violence that finds expression in the books of the Prophets, the burning love of justice, the desperation of the teachers of Jerusalem, the sorrow and the grandeur of the Book of Job, the sensuality of the Song of Songs. All this is in us, all this is in me, and it is the better part of me. This is which I seek to feel within me and to translate in my music.

—*Ernest Bloch*

As a "People of the Book" who pride themselves equally on understanding as well as feeling, Jews are lovers of law, custom, *eruvim* (boundaries), and precise definition. In addition to faith, it is fundamentally important for Jews to understand the genesis and the basis of concepts and to have a secure knowledge of what is "kosher" and what is not.

In Jack Gottlieb's entertaining book, *Funny, It Doesn't Sound Jewish: How Yiddish Songs and Synagogue Melodies Influenced Tin Pan Alley, Broadway and Hollywood* (SUNY Press), the author traces the "Jewish" genesis of many popular song melodies by noted songwriters, including Irving Berlin, George Gershwin, Harold Arlen, and Cole Porter (who was not Jewish)—to Jewish biblical, liturgical, and Yiddish folk roots. After playing through Gottlieb's well-researched, slyly annotated, musical examples and reading his witty commentary, I smiled at Judaism's subtle but certain impact upon our American pop tune culture. For example, I was amused to hear the similarity between *"Rozhenkes Mit Mandlen*—

Raisins and Almonds" and Irving Berlin's *"Blue Skies."* However, I was not quite convinced of the difference between its secular European, immigrant folk roots and what made the cradle song Jewish music.

What is the essence of Jewish music? Why is it always so challenging to answer this question? Don't we know Jewish music when we hear it?

Is it not part of Jewry's visceral, tribal identity and at the very core of the sounds that define us? And, indeed, how can one go about studying Jewish music if one has problems defining it?

The previous chapter outlined the simultaneous traits (or parameters) that comprise music in general, including melody, rhythm, harmony, dynamics, tempo, style, and timbre. These aspects apply to all music from all ages and are universal phenomena.

Is not Jewish music first and foremost music? What characteristics does it have that differentiate it from the universal set? How is Jewish music different than other kinds of music? We listen to Jewish music in the same way that we listen to other kinds of music; music is music—right?

Not quite, there's more to it than that, and here's the rub. First, we must answer the astoundingly complex question of what something means to be "Jewish." Once we add the modifier "Jewish" to music (or anything else), many non-musical issues, including religion, history, geography, sociology, psychology, cultural style, practice, and philosophy come into play.

In other words, if, under all circumstances, you are able to define the essence of a "Jewish" experience to your satisfaction, then that experience's music will be far easier to define as well.

Though we may be conversant with the "how" of musical parameters, we must also become reporters investigating the "who, what, where, when, and why" of Jewish music. That is to say, aside from how it sounds, what non-musical functions or purposes does it fulfill?

In his *Essence of Judaism*, Rabbi Leo Baeck suggests that "All education starts with forbidding." So, perhaps, a way to begin, though a bit negative, is by describing what Jewish music is not. This approach will also make clear to you the difficulties inherent in any one comprehensive definition.

•

1. **Jewish music is not based on any one melody, harmony, rhythm, sound, scale or instrument.**

While there are certain modes and melodic formulas associated with cantillation (chanting of scripture) and nusach (prayer modes), these melodies are not absolute, but change and mutate depending upon who sings them, where, geographically, they are sung, and when in our history they were sung. Defining even codified Jewish music is challenging because of this diverse spectrum of materials and context.

In 1967, Professor Avigdor Herzog, Director of the National Sound Archives in Israel, did a cantillation study at Hebrew University in Jerusalem. He collected recordings of *baalei koreh* (Torah chanters) from many different Jewish communities in both the Ashkenazi and Sephardi synagogues around the world who demonstrated, on recordings, the variations in the public chanting of the first paragraph of Genesis. Depending on the skills of the chanter, the community, the geographic location, and the communication with other communities, using the same text and melodic formula, hundreds of different variations were recorded.

•

2. **Jewish music is not composed and/or performed only by Jewish composers and performers.**

Eighteenth century Italian Catholic Benedetto Marcello's *Ebrai Tedeschi* (An adaptive setting of *Maoz Tzur* – A German Chanukah hymn tune of *Rock of Ages* that he heard in Venice); French Christian Louis Saladin's *Circumcision Cantata,* commissioned by a wealthy Jewish merchant anticipating his yet-to-be-born son's circumcision; German Protestant Max Bruch's variations of the *Kol Nidre* for cello; Basque Catholic Maurice Ravel and Russian Dimitri Shostakovich's *Jewish Folk Songs;* Sergei Prokofiev's *Overture on Hebrew Themes;* Igor Stravinsky's *Abraham and Isaac* (set in Hebrew); or even John William's Holocaust film score theme from *Schindler's List* were not composed or arranged by Jews, but are embraced as Jewish music.

Perry Como and Connie Francis were good Catholics and the Mormon Tabernacle Chorus were good members of the church of Latter Day Saints when they recorded and frequently performed Jewish chants and songs.

•

Max Bruch explained his fascination with the *Kol Nidre* this way in a letter to cantor and musicologist Eduard Birnbaum:

> I became acquainted with Kol Nidre and a few other songs [among others, "Arabian Camel"] in Berlin through the Lichtenstein family, who befriended me. Even though I am a Protestant, as an artist I deeply felt the outstanding beauty of these melodies and therefore I gladly spread them through my arrangement.

Alexander Knapp, a British musicologist, wonders about this same question in his article published in *The Blackwell Companion to Jewish Culture*:

> Would it be true to say that anything composed not by Jews, not for Jews, not as Jews, is *ipso facto* not Jewish music? ...Can we tell, just by listening to Ernest Bloch's *Sacred Service*, that although the composer was Jewish, this work was not parochially conceived, but rather intended as a gift for the whole of humanity? Can we tell, just by listening, that Felix Mendelssohn's *Violin Concerto* was written by a Jewish-born musician who had embraced Christianity? In other words, are genetics and ideology the only criteria for determining Jewishness in music? What about the content and sound of Jewish music, and its appearance when notated? Hugo Weisgall, the important American-Jewish composer and scholar contends in his definition that "there are no specific, objective musical qualities which make a piece Jewish or not."

•

3. All Jewish composers and performers do not create Jewish music.

While one creative ethnomusicologist, Professor Ellen Koskoff of the Eastman School of Music, has suggested that Irving Berlin's *White Christmas* is Jewish because it:

> related his experience as a Jewish immigrant in America to that of many Jewish immigrants in the first half of the twentieth century who helped construct beautiful, hopeful, and essentially tolerant pictures of this country with their musics [sic]. [Tin Pan Alley, Broadway, and the popular music industry, etc. were basically controlled by Jewish immigrants at that time.] I played with the notion that a piece of music [in this case White Christmas], while on the surface seemingly expressing the values of Christianity, is also expressing a nostalgic Jewish immigrant picture of America."

Most other analysts, however, see *White Christmas* as a commercial Christmas song with no identifiable Jewish content or purpose. Bob Dylan, Neil Diamond, and Barry Manilow's albums are not collections of Jewish music, even though these artists are Jewish, have composed these songs, and are performing them.

•

4. **Jewish music is not performed in the same way in different geographic locations.**

Just as melodies, harmonies, and rhythms change geographically, the vocal practices and customs of performers change too. The same melody for *Kol Nidre* will sound different depending upon where it is chanted and by whom. The art of the cantor *(Hazzanut)* depends on how artfully these variations are sung. The same prayer text for the same occasion in the liturgical calendar will sound quite different based on the improvisatory skill of the cantor. The use of vocal colors and ornamentation associated with a region and an artist distinguish one resulting performance from another.

•

5. **Jewish music is not composed and performed similarly by different Jewish sub-groups and communities.**

To understand this wide variance, one only has to listen to the musical differences among Hassidic, Reform, Conservative, Reconstructionist, Humanistic, Persian, Ashkenazi, and Sephardi Jews in America.

Multiply these by the regional differences throughout Jewish communities around the world and you have a tremendously large menu of quite different examples of Jewish music. Interestingly, each Jewish community will inevitably challenge the authenticity of another's version of the same text setting.

•

6. **Jewish music is not composed or performed in the same way that it was seventy-five years ago.**

Even if you geographically isolate any one of the sub-groups mentioned above and contrast their present music with how it was performed fifty or seventy-five years ago, even if it existed at all more than a hundred years ago, you would hear dramatic differences.

For example, only fifty years ago the more formal, choral, organ-accompanied, composed music of the American Reform movement turned one hundred and eighty degrees to an informal, unison, guitar-accompanied, "pop" service music of today.

Even "traditional" *MiSinai* chants, so ancient that these unattributable melodies seem to have been handed down from Mount Sinai, sound different by their musical arrangements from performances recorded fifty years ago.

So, if Jewish music cannot be identified by who wrote it or how it sounds or the way it is performed or where and when we hear it, how are we to determine if it is, indeed, Jewish music and, more importantly, what settings or examples are better than others?

Before intelligent answers can be offered, additional investigative questions must be asked. In this pursuit, each individual Jewish musical work must be scrutinized on its own terms by asking and answering the following questions:

When was it composed?

Where was it first used?

Who first performed it?

Where is it heard today?

What needs were gratified by its creation?

Who performs it and who hears it today?

Why and how is it performed?

What style or multiple styles are reflected in it?

What text does it set?

When, where, and why is the text used?

How does the musical setting illuminate the text?

•

Addressing these questions, the following generalities may be gleaned:

There is no single, identifiable sound to Jewish music.

The composer of Jewish music need not be Jewish, and not every Jewish composer writes Jewish music.

The traditions of style and function in Judaism are not set in stone; they are fluid and constantly changing.

There are many approaches, styles, and fashions in composing Jewish music.

The geography, affiliation, and cultural style of the composer's host country bear directly on the sound and performance practices of Jewish music.

The geographic and historic treatment of Jewry has determined to what extent Jewish music could be created in the recent past.

Where and when texts are found in the worship service also determines how they are set.

•

Appreciating the complexity inherent in any one definition, one ultimately wonders if there are there any yardsticks, aside from Supreme Court Justice Potter Stewart's guideline, "I know it when I see it [or hear it],"that can be used, if not to define, at the very least, to quantify and qualify Jewish musical works. Yes, there are two simple, and workable standards to help us understand the complexity of what makes music Jewish: **function** and *midrash.* The former is easier to understand than the latter.

The Hebrew word for art, *oman* (*Aleph, Mem, Nun*) has the same derivation as amen and the Hebrew word emunah (faith). Art in Jewish life, whether visual or aural, initially aided worship and the pragmatic practice of the religion. Ceremonial art has been around since the artistic thirteen-year-old Betzalel, grandson of Miriam, was commissioned by Moses one year after the Exodus from Egypt to design and create the *Mishkan* (the Tabernacle) in the Sinai Desert.

Today we have *Kiddush* (sanctification of the wine) cups, Sabbath candlesticks, *Kippot,* (skull caps) *Talitot* (prayer shawls), *M'zuzot* (doorpost Scripture containers), *Havdalah* sets (close of Shabbat ceremonial objects), and *Mizrach* plaques (the Easterly direction for prayer) as wonderful examples of visual ceremonial art. One contemporary manufacturer on the West Coast has even concocted Apple and Honey *Piñatas* for Rosh Hashanah!

However, in refuting religious functionality and exploring non-synagogue ritual art, Jewish theatre anthologist and scholar Ellen Schiff has said:

> As to the term "American Jewish play," as I've learned for more than thirty years, it has multiple dimensions and definitions. However, the practice of religious ritual is no more the sole defining criterion for Jewish plays than it is for Jewish life.

In the 2004 *Journal of Judaism and Civilization*, art historian Menahem Alexenberg gave this assessment:

> In the current digital era, we are witnessing the change of art from iconic representation to dialogic presentation, from static image to dynamic process, from passive appreciation to interactive collaboration, and from imitating the creation to imitating the Creator. It is not the vision of a complete and ideal nature to be copied that is the primary artistic value, but it is the continuation of the dynamic process of creation itself that is valued in Judaism.

Functional music attendant to these ceremonies is also plentiful and shares these same ritual possibilities. Listen now to a ceremonial setting of the *Sheva B'rachot* (The Seven Blessings) chanted at Jewish weddings.

•

Play example #3—*Sheva B'rachot* from *Kol Simcha* sung by Cantor Aviva Rosenbloom.

It is fair to say that any music used for a Jewish liturgical, life-cycle ceremony, or holiday celebration is Jewish music because its Jewish function is overt and explicit. However, the quality that makes one example in this genre better than another is the *midrash* inherent in the music, what Alexenberg called the continuation of the dynamic process of creation by artistic interpretation. The uneremonial, less apparent examples of Jewish music, poetic settings, instrumental music and dramatic structures, may also be identified and evaluated by their midrashic content.

Is there a Jewish *midrash* to Irving Berlin's *Easter Parade*? No! Being Jewish is not a prerequisite for composing Jewish music, and there is nothing "Jewish" to understand in the song, which was originally a melody entitled, *Smile and Show Your Dimples*.

Is there a Jewish *midrash* to Igor Stravinsky's *Abraham and Isaac*? Yes, just as one would read a literary collection of *midrashim* in Shalom Spiegel's *The Last Trial* or Alan Dershowitz's commentary of the *Binding of Isaac* in his *The Genesis of Justice*, Stravinsky's musical setting, with correct accentuation in Hebrew, has a point of view. Though composed by a Christian steeped in the Russian Orthodox religion, the musical language does not follow the cantillation but is more abstract, and helps us understand the *Akeida* (the *Binding of Isaac*) in a new, emotional way.

In short, a more productive question to ask is not, "Is it Jewish music?" but, "What is the nature and quality of the *midrash* in the ritual or non-functional Jewish music being studied?"

At lectures, I usually hold up a page of the Talmud as a visual analogy. I point out that the center text in bold is the *Mishneh* and all the Hebrew and Aramaic writings around it, comprising most of the page, are interpretations from various scholars and diverse scholastic periods, offering layers of insight, elucidation, and analytic commentary upon the central idea. If one can identify that bit of *Mishneh* in the center as an essence of Jewish thought, then the Talmud surrounding it is its "Jewish music."

It is not enough for the experience to be provincial, have a cute title, or quote Hebrew or Yiddish words within the lyric. It must elevate the Jewish subject to a new level of understanding and feeling.

Ultimately, when we figure out what it is about an idea that is essentially Jewish, then that entity's musical "Talmud" would be considered Jewish music. It is a simple answer to an extraordinarily complex question and one that leaves both scholars and congregants continuing in their search for a personally satisfying meaning.

•

Chapter 4
What is Traditional *Midrash?*

You shall not add anything to what I command you or take anything away from it, but keep the commandments of the Lord your God that I enjoin upon you.
          —Deuteronomy 4:2

Be deliberate in judgment, raise up many disciples, and make a fence around the Torah.
          —Pirkei Avot – Ethics of the Ancestors

In setting the groundwork for an exploration of Jewish music as *midrash*, we have addressed active listening, the traits of music, and the challenge of distinguishing identifiable "Jewish" aspects of music. We now continue defining terms by offering a basic introduction to traditional literary *midrash* to learn how we can adapt and apply this way of thinking as we listen to *midrashic* Jewish music. For those seeking more than a brief primer on traditional literary *midrash*, Jacob Neusner's book, *What is Midrash?* is highly recommended reading.

Traditional *midrash* is a companion literature of rabbinic interpretation written in a combination of Hebrew and Aramaic, and now English and other languages. It seeks to understand and interpret the law and the lore of the Torah, both written and orally transmitted, by illuminating hidden meanings, suggesting details where specifics are missing, clarifying metaphors, making connections between similarities, justifying repetitions, and resolving discrepancies.

From a historical and political point of view, Rabbi Stephen Pearce points out that the larger purpose of traditional *midrash* was far more than literary interpretation:

> As Judaism transformed from a land-based religion to a text-based religion it also moved law from being Torah and cult centered to rabbi centered, thereby freeing the rabbis from the literal restrictions of the Torah.

Author Al Mellman, in his original *A Radical Approach to Jewish History*, further explains the lack of *midrashim* relating to the *N'viim* (Prophets) as rabbinic de-emphasis of the more land-based writings of the Davidic Prophets and the emphasis of the Torah and the *Megillot* passages used in the evolution of Temple sacrifice in the development of synagogue prayer.

> The rabbis who created the Midrash Rabah used the texts to talk about morality and sin, because Judaism, after the war in 70 CE, was called a *religio licita*, that is a permitted religion of rites, philosophy and laws; but not a nationalism. That is why they did not comment on the Prophets who were nationalists, and that is why when the rabbis at Yavne added the third section of "K'tuvim" [Writings] to the Tanach, their statement in the Talmud is, "No more may be added to the Torah, because the voice of "n'viut" [prophecy] has left Israel." The midrashim as published were also political statements. They are not just lovely stories to entertain Jews at the synagogue. They were to teach a non-nationalistic religion.

The destruction of both temples fundamentally challenged the identity and core relationship that Jews had with God. If conceivable, it must have been an even greater agony for the Jews in Jerusalem to witness the Second Temple being destroyed by the Romans. It was traumatic enough for the First Temple to be demolished and the Ark of the Covenant stolen, but with the second temple, even with the ark absent from within it, the Holy of Holies on the temple mount was God's home, the essential chamber where ancient Jews believed that God dwelt on earth. Only the High Priest was allowed one day a year to enter it, on Yom Kippur, to pray for his people's forgiveness from their sins. The force of God's presence in that room was thought to be so powerful that a rope was tied to the High Priest's leg so that if anything should happen to him while praying for his people, he could be pulled out in time, thus abating God's wrath.

When the second temple and the Holy of Holies was destroyed, where was God to dwell on earth?

The prophet Ezekiel ingeniously answered this, thereby assuaging the anxiety of his people, by saying, "God's presence fills the earth." If God is everywhere, then Judaism could survive the destruction of the Temple and the Holy of Holies. However, there had to be a clear delineation of law, customs, and belief to assure this presence in all parts of the world and our lives. While this knowledge was the priests' responsibility while the Temple stood, now it was to be every Jew's task as instructed by the rabbis. This rabbinic educational mission, clearly delineated as codifying, clarifying, and consummating the Jews' relationship with God, created the *Mishneh* - the Oral Law and all of its elucidations that we label *midrash*.

From a psycho-sociological approach, Dr. Ian Russ sees the value of traditional *midrash* as:

> bridging the gap of time, culture and society between original text, its author, and the person reading the text. Midrash clarifies the context and motivations of the characters and events in the text and the original authors in a manner to give meaning and relevance to the reader today.

From a phenomenological point of view, *midrash* can also be understood as an investigative search (Hebrew: *drash*) to get to know the many sides of a seemingly direct biblical idea (Torah), or the conditions surrounding it, more intimately and authoritatively with both powers of the brain, cognitive and affective.

The continual creation of *midrash* is part of a devotional loyalty and an enduring penchant for re-interpretation that Jews demonstrably have had with their religious and wisdom literature since the Patriarchs shared their own and others' dreams.

Interestingly, while the rabbis sequentially and logically analyze both the oral and written bible, and their communal ramifications throughout the ages, there is more than a slight rabbinic tendency to discourage less cognitive states as a viable alternative to rational interpretations.

While Rabbi Bradley Shavit Artson of the American Jewish University (University of Judaism) refutes this assessment by advocating studying Talmud as poetry, traditionally, throughout the ages, the rabbis have been far more comfortable with the scientific approach of proof texts and applied logic than the alternatives of free, affective association.

Traditionally there were two kinds of interpretive literature. *Midrash* is divided into *Midrash Halachah* (Hebrew: the way to "walk" or travel through life, via laws and statutes) and *Midrash Haggadah* (Hebrew: to talk or narrate a story by employing aphorisms, homilies, and folklore).

The highly cognitive, legalistic *Midrash Halachah* utilizes several scholarly techniques in its rational approach. The genre interprets scripture (hermeneutics), explains religious texts through definition, grammatical usage, and syntax (exegesis), employs practical rules of thumb, probability and common sense (heuristics), and even enters into the philosophical world of epistemology (probing what distinguishes true from false knowledge). *Halachah* can be questioned.

Midrash Halachah is considered in a parallel universe, with the written law and *Torah Shebe'al Peh* the Oral Law that was transmitted to the authors of the *Mishnah* and then further considered through discussion by the Talmudists.

There are three books of *Halachic* (legal) *midrashim* (pl.) The *Mechilta* (*The Measure*) for the book of *Shemot* (Exodus), the *Torat Kohanim* (*The Law of the Priests*) for the book of *VaYikra* (Leviticus) and the *Sifre (The Two Books)* for the books of *BaMidbar* (Numbers) and *Devarim* (Deuteronomy). There is no *Halachic* book of *midrashim* for *B'reishit* (Genesis), as there were no applicable laws within it that needed to be interpreted.

With the Babylonian exile in 587-539 BCE, rabbinic Judaism needed to replace nationalism with religious universality. They changed *Moshe N'vieinu* (Moses our Prophet) to *Moshe Rabbeinu* (Moses our Teacher). Geography was replaced with ideas and deeds.

As rabbinic authority evolved, the pursuit of Halachic understanding and adherence to the Torah through codification became essential. Highly structured principles of reason (*midot*) arose to gird this structure. An early system of seven rational interpretative rules was organized by a Babylonian rabbi, Hillel the Elder:

The Seven Rules of Hillel *haZaken* (the Elder) – 1st century BCE

1. *Kal vachomer* (light and heavy). That which applies in a less important case will apply in a more important case, and vice versa. For example, if an act is forbidden on an ordinary festival then it is also forbidden on Yom Kippur. The reverse applies. If an act is permitted on Yom Kippur, then it is permitted on an ordinary festival.

2. *Gezeirah shavah* (equivalence of expressions). An analogy can be made between two separate texts on the basis of a similar phrase, word, or root.

For example Exodus 21:2 says "Hebrew slave" and from Deuteronomy 14:12 where it says, "If your Hebrew brother is sold to you," we infer that "Hebrew slave" means a slave who is a Hebrew as opposed to a Hebrew who owns a slave.

3. *Binyan av* (a principle cited in several passages). A consideration found in one passage applies to all of them.

4. *K'lal ufrat* (the general and the particular). A general principle may be restricted by a more detailed description of it in another verse.

5. *Sh'nei ketuvim* (a standard derived from two passages). Two laws may be related together to form a principle, which then can be used to interpret other laws.

6. *Keyotzei bo mimakom acher* (like that in another place). An explanation of a word in one text can be clarified by use of same word in an unrelated text.

7. *Davar halameid mi'inyano* (a definition formed from context). The total context, not just the isolated statement, must be considered for an accurate interpretation.

To demonstrate how deeply detailed the legalistic, cognitive roots of *halachic midrash* were, the system of seven *midot* did not suffice. Techniques of logic used in investigative interpretation later expanded and developed into:

•

The Thirteen Midot (Rules) of Rabbi Yishmael - 2nd century BCE

1. A conclusion may be drawn from a minor premise to a major one, or from a more lenient one to a stricter one, and vice versa.

2. A conclusion may be drawn from an analogy between two laws based on identical expressions in the biblical text.

3. A conclusion may be drawn from a general principle as found in one or in two related biblical texts that becomes applicable in all similar cases, even if not specifically described in detail.

4. A conclusion may be drawn from a rule followed by an explicit case. It then only applies to that particular.

5. A conclusion may be drawn when a specification is followed by a general rule. Everything in that general rule then applies.

6. A conclusion may be drawn from a general rule that is followed by a specification and then followed by a general rule and is then applicable only to such cases that are similar to the specifics.

7. A conclusion may be drawn from a general rule requiring an explicit specification.— for the sake of clarity, rule 4 applies, and a specification requiring a general rule — again, for the sake of clarity, rule 5 applies).

8. A conclusion may be drawn from every particular included in a general law and singled out to instruct us concerning something new, and is done so not just to teach us its own case, but to be applied to the whole of the general law.

9. Every particular case included in a general law that is singled out to add a different provision similar to the general law is done so as to lessen, not to increase, the severity of the provision.

10. Every particular case included in a general law that is singled out to add a different provision that is unlike the general provision, is singled out in order to, sometimes, lessen or to, sometimes, add to the severity of the provision.

11. Every particular case included in a general law that is singled out by a new stipulation, the provisions within the general law no longer apply to it, except where the Torah says that they do.

12. The meaning of a passage may be deduced from its own context or from a subsequent passage.

13. Similarly, when two passages contradict each other, the meaning can be clarified with a proof of a third (biblical) text, which reconciles them.

These thirteen principles of interpretation were affirmed and said to be part of the Oral Law dating back to the written law *Chumshei Torah* (The Five Books of Moses); Rabbi Ishmael merely defined and wrote them down. We remind ourselves of them as a way of viewing the world each day as we read them, as part of the liturgy, in our preparatory morning prayers.

From seven to thirteen *midot,* the systematic progression of interpretation, ever-mindful of the rabbi's growing legalistic worldview, ultimately grows in sophistication and complexity to the *32 Rules of Rabbi Eliezer ben Yosi haGalili* – later in the 2nd century.

All three guides are found in the *Baraitot,* (external teachings outside of the *Mishneh*) authored by the Jewish sages (*Tannaim*) of the period from Hillel, 100 BCE, when the *Tanach* (Acronym for *Torah, Prophets and Writings*) was finalized, to the compilation of the *Mishneh,* 200 CE. Together the *Mishneh*—core topics organized in six orders and each order into tractates include:

Zeraim (Seeds). 11 tractates. Agricultural laws and prayers

Moed (Festival). 12 tractates. Laws of the Sabbath and the Festivals

Nashim (Women). 7 tractates. Laws of marriage and divorce

Nezikin (Damages). 10 tractates. Civil and criminal law

Kodshim (Holy things). 11 tractates. Sacrificial rites, the Temple, and dietary laws

Tohorot (Purities). 12 tractates. Laws of purity and impurity, including the impurity of the dead, the laws of ritual purity for the *Kohanim* (priests), and the laws of "family purity" (the menstrual laws); and the

Gemara (the surrounding discussions of the *Mishneh*) comprise the *Talmud*.

These methods result in interpretations and parallel insights that are given equal weight by the rabbis with the oral law and, together, form the basis for all subsequent rabbinic discussion in the *Gemara* (complete discussion), 200-500 CE.

The *Amoraim* (sages of the Gemara) succeeded the *Tanna'im*.

Even with these highly cognitive, sequentially structured, *midot*, different schools of thought, the Academies of Hillel and Shamai being the most well-known, did not always agree on common critical criteria. While Shamai's academy sought purity and exactness, Hillel's disciples were more pragmatic and flexible in their viewpoints. This philosophical variance is found in constructive argumentation between the two schools that has illuminated the Talmud and resulted in opposing interpretations.

After the second century, in contrast with this progressively complex legalistic method of inquiry, a more individualistic, narrative, and free body of interpretation known as *Midrash Haggadah* dealing with biblical lore developed. *Midrashic* expositions of both kinds appeared throughout the Talmud, but the increasing trend of balancing cognitive proof texts with freely associative, homiletic, descriptions and storytelling continued into the Middle Ages and, in one literary form or another, continue evolving down to the present.

Midrash Haggadah, the non-legal side of Jewish awareness, has the luxury of being less rigid and more poetically intuitive in its narrative techniques. On most occasions today, when *midrash* is referred to and cited, it is not from the *Midrash Halachah*, since the Talmud has incorporated so much of it, but from the *Midrash Haggadah* or *Aggadot*.

Kollel: The Adult Centre for Liberal Jewish Learning offers this example of *Midrash Haggadah*:

> The Torah says (Lev. 23:39) to live in a *sukkah*, [a booth or temporary hut during the Festival of Tabernacles], but there is no indication of what a *sukkah* should look like; it says to take branches and fruit and be happy, but it's very unclear what kind of branches or fruit, or what to do with them.

> However, people certainly were building *sukkot* [pl.] and waving branches; traditions had developed about how to do these things. The Rabbis studied the Torah to "search out" ways in which the traditions of how to do things were already hinted at, and answers to questions they still had about the right way to do things. By reading closely and carefully, they found answers: for example, the Hebrew letters of the word "*sukkah*", *Samekh, Khaf,* and *Hei,* tell us that a *sukkah* can be completely enclosed, like a *Samekh,* or have three walls and an open side, like a *Khaf,* or have two full walls and a partial wall, like a *Hei.*

The body of *Midrash Hagg*adah begins with the first book of the Torah (*B'reishit*) and runs through it in order. The most important sources for these are found in the *Midrash Rabbah* (The Great Midrash), a collection of commentaries on the Torah and the Five *Megillot* (Scrolls -- the Song of Songs, Esther, Ruth, Lamentations, Ecclesiastes), and the *Pesikta Midrashim* (Divisions), concerning the Festivals. It does not include the Prophets. This body of rabbinic literature contains the earliest exploratory thought in the Jewish tradition.

•

There is a third stream of "popular" *midrash* that bridges the rabbinic traditional literature with modern times and is vibrantly alive and still being written and published today.

Lay authors, philosophers, and even communal and political observers offer it. Consider part of the mission statement of a recent on-line computer journal devoted to modern *midrash* disseminated on the Internet:

Modern Midrash is the online journal of AJCOP, the professional association for the advancement of community organization practice, affiliated with the Jewish Communal Service Association. AJCOP is dedicated to the development, enhancement and strengthening of the professional practice of Jewish community service.

> *Modern Midrash* is devoted to fostering community, dialogue and learning among AJCOP colleagues. The journal will explore issues related to the continuity, well being and survival of the Jewish people; the welfare of the Jewish community, its organizations and individuals; Jewish identity; Jewish ethics, morals, culture, history, tradition and religious values; the special relationship between Israel and the Jewish Diaspora; the theory and practice of community organization; professional training and continuing education; the application of the values that mark our field, such as *tzedek/tzedakah/chesed, limud*, and *tikkun olam* (justice, philanthropy, compassion, learning, and social action); Jewish social issues; and communal policy. The Journal will be especially attuned to discussions of the ethical and values issues that are embedded in Jewish community organization practice.

Another interesting website to visit is "Virtual Talmud – Rabbi's Blog for the Sake of Heaven," an interesting point/counterpoint *midrashic* approach to modern issues that culls its authority from traditional literature.

For our study, traditional literary *midrash* is instructive in its ideas and techniques. By adapting them, creating new approaches and musical applications, we can use the two sides of the genre, like the two aspects of our brain, to understand a new body of musical *midrash*.

This artistic *beraita* (teaching outside of the *mishnah* or mainstream) is yet another way of "re-booting" *midrashic* interpretive possibilities and powers of commentary. It allows visual, aural, and performing artists to connect with existing literary midrash as students and offer, in turn, their own insights through their art, incorporating it as another facet of the larger, ongoing body of *Midrash Haggadah*.

As effective musical *midrash*, the composer first asks: How can this music interpret the text or idea? What hidden meanings, unspecified details, un-interpreted metaphors, unmade connections, unresolved discrepancies or contradictions between intellect and emotion can music create by its skillful inclusion and setting?

Consider, for a moment, any one of the unfulfilled circumstances listed above as the visual footage of a silent film. The protagonist or intellectual issue is established; the environment or context is delineated; and, yet, the entire expressive impact is somehow missing.

For example: We see a man with a neutral expression leaving a building with a package. He looks around and then gets into a car and drives away.

A composer about to underscore this scene might well wonder:

What or who was in that building?

What was in that package?

When he looked around, who was he looking for?

What was his state of mind when he left the building?

Where is he driving to in his car?

•

Appropriate, artful music can suggest several supportive interpretive scenarios to this missing information as *midrash*.

If the underscore music is optimistic it might suggest that the package could be a gift that the man had obtained in the building. Was it a store?

Perhaps, since the man looked around, it might be a surprise present. The music suggests that he is emotionally buoyant, optimistic, and could well be going in his car to his father, mother, child, or sweetheart, to give them the present.

If the music is tragically sad it might suggest that the package could contain something of remains -- either papers or, even, an urn of ashes. Was the building a government office or a mortuary?

When he looks around, perhaps he is ashamed to let people see his wretched condition or feelings. Could it be that he is going in his vehicle to bury these remains, or safely deposit them for later reflection? If they are papers, how will these affect him?

If the music is agitated or malevolent, it may very well reflect his state of mind as he leaves the building with something equally evil and harmful. Was the building a hideout? Looking around, he certainly wouldn't want witnesses. Could it be stolen goods, a weapon, or secret plans to destroy something big and important? Is he on his way to carry out this treacherous plan?

Though none of these scenarios are conclusive, they each provide an additional emotional context and, thereby, offer a plausible, enrichment of an interpretive direction. The likelihood of that interpretation being the most meaningful depends on the skill of the film composer, as it would the rabbinic scholar offering a literary *midrash*.

•

But music is not only about mood. Melodies, rhythms, harmonies, and textures also carry resonance with music that has already been heard. Often these stored musical stimuli in our data banks recall a similar setting from a scenario that might shed light on the present one.

The musical setting might sound like an analogous song containing a lyric that is evocative of a deeper sense. Perhaps, the music suggests a personal experience that you thought was disconnected from the consideration at hand, but now seems to inform the present issue.

•

Jewish liturgical, life cycle, biblical, dramatic, and poetic musical settings that I have composed will be presented in succeeding chapters and offered as examples of my process and interpretation of each text's setting. If the musical *midrash* is convincing, you will hear, understand, and know the intellectual and emotional issues of the text differently and more comprehensively by accepting and adding its musical import into the equation. Listening to and reading about these compositions will enable you to understand how visual, aural, and performing arts are affective and, at the very least, equally as capable and insightful as traditional literary forms of *midrash.*

It is only because of the traditional rabbinic proscription of *avodah zarah* (idol worship) that art and music, outside of basic ceremonial functions, have not been previously discussed in *midrashic* terms. The second commandment forbidding idol worship has even the rabbis in a quandary. Lionel Kochan, in his book, *Beyond the Graven Image: A Jewish View,* believes that artistic idolatry was only applied to visual experiences, not the auditory.

Menahem Alexenberg, in his upcoming book on Semiotics, develops the idea that the sages could not even conceptualize music as art until very much later. However, together with the literary tradition, in a modern context, *midrashic* music can provide greater clarity to Jewish texts, perceptions, communal and individual life experiences, and an elevated appreciation of God's presence and meaning in our collective and personal lives.

•

Chapter 5
The *Midrash* of the Orchard

Better to lease one garden and cultivate it than to lease many and neglect them. As the proverb goes: who leases a garden eats birds; who leases gardens is eaten by birds.
—*Ecclesiastes Rabbah*

In *Talmud Bavli* (the Babylonian Talmud, compiled in the sixth century CE), in section *Chagigah* 14, a story is told of four *Tanna'im* (scholars in the generation after the destruction of the second temple) who studied laws of the supernatural and entered a mystical *pardes*. Literally, in Hebrew, a *pardes* is an orchard or a garden. Additionally, the word's sound suggests its metaphoric meaning of Paradise, a Garden of Eden. The Hebrew word is also an acronym used in *Midrash*:

PaRDeS

P—corresponding to the Hebrew letter *pei,* stands for *pshat,* (simple, direct meaning).

R—corresponding to the Hebrew letter, *reish,* stands for *remez,* a hinted-at hidden meaning.

D—corresponding to the Hebrew letter, *dalet,* stands for *drush* (the root of the word *drash* and *midrash*), an interpretive meaning derived at by various *halachic* and/or *aggadic* techniques.

S—corresponding to the Hebrew letter, *samach,* stands for *sod,* a "secret" or subconscious meaning that surfaces through introspection and meditation.

The story goes that of the four scholars who entered the *pardes* "orchard," which in its "sod" or "secret" aspect must have involved entering a state resembling intense meditation, the only one who emerged unscathed was Rabbi Akivah, who was forty years old, life experienced, deeply in love with his wife, and happily married. The other three, who were less balanced and more obsessed in their journey, became heretics, were stricken insane, or died.

The inference is that any system that is not "entered into" and studied with balance, focus, perspective, preparation, and an "exit strategy" can be taken to its unproductive, if not unhealthy, extreme.

These four levels of understanding have also been associated with the four main areas of rabbinic study:

Pshat – The primary, literal source of **Torah**

Remez – Complementary aspects of meaning found in the **Mishneh**

Drash – The *halachic* and *aggadic* interpretive discussions in the **Talmud**

Sod – The mystical meanings in occult literature collectively called **Kabbalah**

Pardes has come to mean four levels of any interpretive inquiry, from the obvious to the esoteric essence of an idea. Considering Jewish music as *midrash,* we can also create a hierarchy of *Pardes* musical meanings that can be employed in discerning the gradations of meaning in the music/text relationship.

Knowing of these levels and identifying their *midrashic* hierarchy helps the listener to understand simultaneous relationships. This idea of simultaneity will be discussed in more detail in the next chapter.

In its musical context, **Pshat** connotes the obvious intellectual and emotional character of the text (happy, sad, energetic, meditative, etc.) with the music in tandem. They are the same.

Not much has to be said about *Pshat* except that, after our awareness that music actually exists as a man-made considered adjunct to the text, and not just some mindless *manna* from heaven, this is the level in which we all enter the "orchard".

From early childhood we learn holiday songs and didactic text memorization tunes using this simple, clear, "What you hear is what you get"-style of setting.

At this entry level, many of us come to believe that all Jewish music is either slow, filled with hard to pronounce Hebrew words, and in a minor (a sad) key or, to the other extreme, as in the "specialty" services so in vogue today, incessantly bouncy, rhythmic, repetitive, constantly happy, and mindlessly youthful. Jewish music at this level is usually clichéd and less engrossing but, like a good soldier, in a *pshat* manner, it serves the basic purpose of enlistment.

In the past forty years, the American Jewish camping movement has produced a body of songs that continues this surface relationship with Jewish texts by keeping congregants adolescents (or younger) as we go about memorizing the words to brief texts, slogans, aphorisms, and the like. The structure of a song (as opposed to a composition) in its brevity, repetition, and expressive limitations promotes a child-like *Pshat* understanding of texts. While camp songs are appropriate for children and teen-agers, they are entry level, least considered, fast food that precludes more adult, nutritious, *midrashic* musical settings.

•

Remez, the less obvious, "hidden", allegoric level of musical and textual understanding, usually occurs when either or both elements are presented in an unexpected way. For example, if a happy idea is set with sad music (or a sad idea with happy music) a light goes on in our heads asking, "Why this juxtaposition?" Something is not quite right. There is an indirectness that is both mildly disquieting and, at the same time, intriguing. We need to pause for a moment and figure out why these elements are married to each other in this way. Martin Buber observes, *"All journeys have secret destinations of which the traveler is unaware."* In the process of unearthing the hidden aspect of meaning, and placing this odd object in a new light, one is the beneficiary of a flash of insight that brings new understanding to either component or the larger construct.

•

Drash brings in a third element to the text/music midrashic amalgam. It is the composer's singular interpretive viewpoint, or conclusion, in the form of a musical homily. Of the many possible interpretations of a text (moral, linguistic, historic, ethical, aesthetic, numerical, etc.), the composer's music reflects a clear, emotive viewpoint. It is a compelling musical realization that warrants our attentive consideration to that subjectively creative opinion.

There is no single way of interpreting anything, and there are certainly many ways of musically setting a text. It is this variety of possible *midrashic* interpretations that have sustained the Jewish people and maintained the greatness of our source material, making it universal and personal at the same time. When the music used in a setting is as intellectually or as emotionally interesting as the text is, and makes us think while we feel, there is a *midrash* to the setting. Those who would rather not think as much as they feel often criticize this music as too "intellectual." They prefer *pshat* interpretations that ask that they only use half (or less) of the brain that God gave them.

•

Sod connotes a newly found deeper, more personal, sometimes esoteric, insight. It is a revelation derived from the elevated synergy of the text and the music as they intersect with our individual dynamics. The *Sefer Zohar* (a Kabbalistic primary source) commenting on Genesis 12:10 teaches:

> Come… come see every place, every moment
> Each and every thing contains secret wisdom.

It is the central issue that clarifies all of our peripheral efforts to fully understand or, as American poet Robert Frost succinctly put in this telling couplet from *A Secret Sits:*

> We dance round in a ring and suppose,
> But the secret sits in the middle and knows.

Sod is the most profound ("secret") level of understanding that is attained from the fullest consideration of the music, text, and our dream state. We network our data bank of emotional experiences to the musical setting of the text. In contradiction to Rav Kook's observation in his book *HaMahshaba HaYisraelit* that man is by nature a mystic, not many listeners are able or care to reach this depth.

It is a risky place to arrive at, because it involves yielding the rabbinic preference for cognitive control. In this "magical" realm one opens oneself to a sensual, emotional awakening that equally informs.

This "complete brain" understanding accesses interpretations that are visceral (intuitive), personal, and insightfully reveal the most affecting aspect of the text-musical setting's construct message. To achieve this most profound state of both intellectual and emotional awareness takes time, patience, and even a surrendering of initially safe intellectual faculties. One often feels the message before understanding it, and feeling deeply about anything in our urgent contemporary society opens us up to risks and personal revelations that we might prefer to avoid. Still, *Sod* is the ultimate awareness.

It is the sum total of all the steps that precede it. It is not for everyone, but for those who are insatiable to know and understand on the deepest level it is the destination and the ultimate reason for the journey.

•

With this *pardes* hierarchy in mind, let us consider ways of interpreting the evening prayer *Hashkiveinu*. The Hebrew text reads:

Hashkiveinu Adonai Eloheinu l'shalom, v'ha-amideinu malkeinu l'chayim,

Grant that we may lie down in peace, Eternal God, and raise us up, O Sovereign, to life renewed.

ufros aleinu sukkat sh'lomecha, v'tak'neinu b'eitzah tovah mil'fanecha, v'hoshieinu l'ma-an sh'mecha.

Spread over us the shelter of Your peace; guide us with your good counsel, and for Your name's sake, be our Help.

V'hagein ba-adeinu, v'haseir me'aleinu oyev, dever v'cherev v'ra-av v'yagon, v'haseir Satan mil'faneinu u-mei-achareinu,

Shield us from hatred and plague; keep us from war and famine and anguish; subdue our inclination to do evil (literally: Keep us from Satan).

uvtzeil k'nafecha tastireinu, ki Eil shom'reinu u-matzileinu atah, ki Eil melech chanun v'rachum atah.

O God, our Guardian and Helper, our gracious and merciful Sovereign, give us refuge in the shadow of Your wings.

Ushmor tzeiteinu u-vo-einu, l'chayim ulshalom mei-atah v'ad olam, [added on Shabbat) ufros aleinu sukkat sh'lomecha.

O guard our coming and our going, that now and always we have life and peace.

Baruch atah Adonai, haporeis sukkat shalom aleinu, v'al kol amo Yisrael, v'al Yerushalayim. Amen

We praise You, O God, whose shelter of Peace is spread over us, over all Your people Israel, and over Jerusalem. *Amen.*

•

As a reminder of the dual nature of literary *midrash,* and how two sides of the brain are used in interpreting this prayer, traditionally, we could employ either the Halachic route and interpret the legalities as Rabbi Daniel Z. Feldman does here in the beginning of a "mini –*shiur*" (mini-lesson) on the Gamara *B'rachot* (Blessings):

> The Talmud states that one who is reciting nighttime *K'riat Sh'ma* (recitation of the Sh'ma) at the very end of its time period should not say *Hashkiveinu.* The Rashba and the Rosh (acronyms of two Talmudic scholars) quote an opinion that this does not refer to the *b'rakhah* (the blessing) itself, which still must be said, but only the actual words referring to "lying down", which are no longer applicable at that time. This implies that while those words are incongruous, the *b'rakhah* itself is an integral part of the structure.

Or we could employ a psychological - *aggadic* viewpoint from the *Being Jewish* Winter 2001 excerpt of Dr. Leonard Felder's *Seven Prayers That Can Change Your Life*,

> Especially in light of the events of September 11, … one prayer you may find useful and comforting… is the *Hashkiveinu*... As you say this prayer, imagine yourself connecting with the mysterious and infinite source of life — the source that keeps your heart beating and your soul pulsing even as you sleep. Think about the truly wonderful phenomenon that our lives and energy continue as we sleep. We inhale and exhale and our hearts continue to beat even when we let go of conscious control and drift off to sleep…

> Each time you say the *Hashkiveinu* prayer at the end of the day, notice if you are still trying to control too much or if you are willing to let go to a comforting feeling or presence that stays with you as you sleep. This is the crucial part of the *Hashkiveinu* prayer that helps us gently enter the world of sleep and dreams.

•

Jewish music as *midrash* offers us a third approach:

Pshat – The text itself without the music is straightforward in its supplication for safety under God's protection while asleep during the night. It might be called the less frightening Jewish version of the children's bedtime prayer:

> "Now I lay me down to sleep, I pray the Lord my soul to keep. If I should die before I wake, I pray the Lord my soul to take. God bless (list of loved ones)…"

The music chosen for the *Pshat* setting mirrors the text in a direct, parallel function as a film score for a cartoon mirrors its action and the mood (this scoring technique is whimsically known as "Mickey Mousing" for example Mickey hits his head and a cowbell is struck to match the action). There is nothing in the music that is surprising. It is utilitarian. For example when the text speaks of evil, the music becomes more menacing.

Remez – The music, at first hearing, seems oblique or opposite of what we would expect from a literal setting. We wonder why the composer chose to set the text in this way. Then, as the music unfolds, we observe a musical trait that illuminates some less considered aspect of the text. Suddenly, the music that seemed unusual takes on a mantle of significance and appropriateness. It colors the text in a revealing hue. A less obvious, hidden meaning reveals itself.

Drash – Instead of the text driving the music or the music "serving" the basic needs of the text, the music takes on equal stature with the words. By its chiseled melody, harmony, etc. it expresses a standpoint that stands on its own. A synergy with an engaging personality emerges, informing us by fusing both the words and music into a new entity – a composition.

Sod – Beginning as a drash, it goes further. A musical resonance, association, or color fragment from the setting triggers a deeper awareness in us that accesses unplanned and unrelated personal cognitive and sense memories. This surprise stimulus transports us to a place within our personal world. Temporarily leaving the interpretation of the text, we seek insight into unresolved personal fears, anxieties, loves, and hopes. We take a mystical flight, an out of body experience, a reverie. We are simultaneously listening to the text setting while on a mystical journey of inner space. As a result of this mysterious bi-level excursion we return understanding the text and ourselves better and more comprehensively.

•

It is significant to note that not every measure of a musical text setting stays on the same level. It may begin as *pshat*, ascend to *midrash*, descend to *remez*, and, if the listener and the music are in synchronization, attain the heights of *sod*. In fact, if the music stayed on one level for too long, it might bore us (*pshat*) or overwhelm us (*sod*). The best settings are like golf games. The strategies of strokes and clubs vary taking us to an ultimately rewarding conclusion.

•

Let us now apply these Pardes levels of musical interpretation as we listen to a musical setting of *Hashkivenu* in recorded example #4 for solo voice and solo bassoon.

In the evening liturgy, *Hashkiveinu* is found in the middle of the service. The compilers of the *siddur* (ordered book of prayers) were careful not to program this petition too early in our devotion to prepare us for the drama of this prayer.

Here is an anecdotal running description of this musical setting with its possible interpretive pardes levels:

Play example #4 *Hashkiveinu* from *Nishmat Chayim, a Sabbath Eve Service* sung by Cantor Faith Steinsnyder

1. A solo bassoon begins playing quietly in a vocal style (what we identify later as the *Hashkiveinu* fragment).

Remez – What is a solo bassoon doing accompanying a prayer? It must represent another voice – Whose?

2. The cantor begins intoning *Hashkiveinu* as the bassoon sustains long notes.

Pshat – clear-cut accompaniment support

3. Bassoon answers the word *chayim* (life) again in the vocal style.

Drash – The instrument affirms and agrees on life's centrality by repeating the *l'chayim* motive and adding a slight discourse.

4. Cantor chants alone unaccompanied until *v'hagein baadeinu* (shield us from our enemies).

Sod – The cantor stops and enables us, in the interim, to consider alternatives (making peace) with the enemies in our life.

5. The bassoon reiterates his first statement and the mood changes.

Sod – In effect, the bassoon continues underscoring our brief trip of introspection.

6. The cantor dramatically lists the evils that could happen as the bassoon answers with short, sharp interjections.

Pshat – parallel statements and response

7. A recurring note in the bassoon accompanies *uv'tzeil k'nafecha tastireinu* (give us refuge in the shadow of Your wings).

Drash – The bassoon provides a persistent *pedal point* (one note ostinato) wall of belief that is our refuge casting a protective shadow over and around us.

8. The bassoon suddenly is silent while the cantor sings alone *chanun v'rachum atah* (You are a gracious and merciful God) the bassoon then affirms it poignantly in its higher, lyrical range.

Sod – Again we are given, through silence, a moment to meditate on God's love and what the price of it has been through the ages.

9. The cantor chants under a long tone until the bassoon stops at the word *shalom* (peace).

Drash – We allow ourselves to hear *shalom* (peace) in the silence of our hearts hoping for *shaleim* (completeness) between the sounds of the world.

10. The cantor continues alone until *meiatah v'ad olam* (now and always).

Drash – Silence enables us to perceive eternity.

11. The bassoon reiterates the *v'ad olam* (eternally) motive as the cantor continues with *sukkat sh'lomecha*.

Drash –The tabernacle of peace is our recurring eternal hope and prayer.

12. As the cantor sings *sukkat sh'lomecha* (tabernacle of Your peace) the bassoon re-enters restating the *Hashkiveinu* fragment.

Drash – We lie down each night meditating on its establishment.

13. Under a long supportive bassoon note the cantor intones the concluding blessing *Baruch Atah*…(Blessed are You).

Pshat – A utilitarian accompaniment.

14. The bassoon is silent under *V'al Y'rushalayim* (and over Jerusalem).

Sod – Jerusalem's vulnerability is a metaphor for our own. Will we ever feel totally safe?

15. The bassoon states the *Hashkiveinu* fragment one last time and then cadences alone with a perfect octave.

Sod – The solo instrument provides bookends of underscoring assuring us (and enabling us to assure ourselves) that a perfect God was with us at the beginning, continues to be in the present, and will be there for us until the very end. We can lie down and sleep secure in that belief.

Each time this setting is performed, I am struck by how quiet the congregation becomes. At first engaged by the novelty of the solo bassoon within a sacred service, by the conclusion of this setting, they understand that the bassoon is that still small voice of Godliness within each of us. Call it religious awareness, conscience or subconscious, it is the non-literary *midrashic* accompaniment that informs, interprets, supports, and completes us as the Oral Law compliments the Torah. We no longer feel isolated from our Source.

Abraham Joshua Heschel beautifully wrote in *Man is Not Alone:*

As long as we see only objects we are alone. When we begin to sing, we sing for all things. Essentially music does not describe that which is; rather it tries to convey that which reality stands for. The universe is a score of eternal music, and we are the cry, we are the voice.

Reason explores the laws of nature, trying to decipher the scales without grasping the harmony, while the sense of the ineffable is in search of the song. When we think, we employ words or symbols of what we feel about things. When we sing, we are carried away by our wonder, and acts of wonder are signs or symbols of what all things stand for.

To this I would add: Think, sing, and think while you sing embracing music as *midrash* in the *Pardes* that is our lives. One does not need to preclude the other. It is in this way that Rabbi Dov Baer; the Maggid of Mezritch's observation may become an active part of our personal and communal Jewish life:

People's good deeds are used by the Eternal as seeds for planting trees in the Garden of Eden: thus, each of us creates our own Paradise.

•

Chapter 6
The *Midrash* of a Single Tone

I have discovered that it is enough when a single note is beautifully played.

—*Composer Arvo* Pärt *from* "Tabula Rasa," *1984*

At first it does not seem natural to play an unwavering tone on a blown or bowed instrument, or to sing one…Now, after forty years of learning to sing long tones, singing them defines my life. They tell me I have a brain that works, ears that hear my voice, and – somewhere - an ideal of perfection.

—"ON TONES" from *The Musical Life* by W. A. Mathieu

There is a midrashic way to perceive music that goes beyond literalism to a place of appreciating music as metaphor. For the generative composer, the interpretive conductor, and emotive performer, and, most of all, for the active listener, it is this midrashic way of embracing the aural world that makes the difference between just pleasant, or nice, and extraordinary! Here is an example:

In music, the songs we sing are made up of a string of single pitches, or tones that each contribute to the totality we call a melody. We can either describe a melody in aggadic terms with general images (lilting, bittersweet, energetic, optimistic, etc.) or, in a halachically structured analysis, as musicologists do. We can be more precise in our terminology, talking about the component tones and their intervallic relationships (the distance between one tone and another).

The interval system is rather straightforward. In a C major scale at the piano we play: C D E F G A B C. We count the name of the scale (in this case C) as a first step and count up to the next desired tone. If C were the first step, the adjacent D, the next piano key up, would be the second, and so that interval is a called a second. C to E would be a third, C to F a fourth, C to G a fifth, C to A a sixth, C to B a seventh, and C to C an octave (an eighth).

Using more specific musical midot we can further qualify intervals by how many half steps comprise the distance between those intervals.

The interval of an octave, fourth, or fifth can further be identified as either being diminished (the closest in distance to each other), perfect, or augmented (the furthest away from each other).

The interval of a second, third, sixth, or seventh can be qualified as diminished (the closest), minor, major, or the furthest in distance—augmented. Before we get too complicated, let's go back to the very beginning to consider a single tone...or what we perceive to be a single tone.

Have you ever considered what makes the tone Middle C on the piano (the C under the name of the piano brand), sound different than the same tone played on a violin or clarinet? Though the pitch is the same, the tonal color is quite different.

The differences lie in an acoustic phenomenon known as the Fundamental and Partial system, or more popularly labeled the Overtone System. Here's how it works: Every tone begins as a vibrating column of air, either set in motion by a hammer striking a wire (piano); a stick or a mallet hitting a skin, wood, or metal (percussion); blown air into a pipe or reed (woodwind); lips vibrating air through a mouthpiece (brass);or vocal chords (voice) vibrating in the throat. The result is a musical sound that has an identifiable pitch and timbre (color).

Tones start their lives as either the lowest fundamental tone of a series of vibrations or an auxiliary member of a group of overtones set in motion by another fundamental vibration. For example: If you strike a low C (two octaves below middle C) on the piano, you might think you are only hearing that low C, but, in reality, while you are hearing that fundamental tone the loudest, you are also hearing its accompanying partial tones that include:

The fundamental C,

C a perfect octave above that,

G a perfect fifth above that,

C (another reinforcing C—middle C)—a perfect fourth above that,

E a major third above that,

Another G a minor third above that,

An out-of-tune B flat a smaller minor third above that,

A fourth reinforcing C a major second above that,

D a major second above that.

E a major second above that,

F sharp a major second above that,

G a minor second above that...

And even more tones that dogs hear better than we do.

The Overtone System
(More correctly - The Fundamental and Partial System)

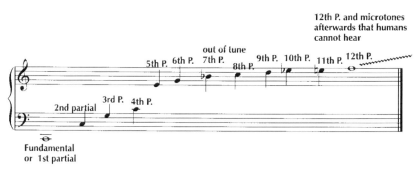

Each continuing overtone partial in the series is a smaller interval apart from the last and slightly less audible. Even more microtones exist in the series but are inaudible to the human ear. It may also be observed that the stability, strength, and direct influence of overtones decreases as they get farther away from their source: the fundamental.

Just as there are really no individual colors, but segments of an ever blending, never ending rainbow, there are really no individual sounds, but combinations of sounds that create the illusion of an isolated entity or source.

The color of a tone (that which makes that middle C on the piano sound different than a middle C played on the violin), aside from the material it is resonating upon and how that material is activated, has to do with how loud and subordinate the fundamental and partials are in relationship to themselves. This ratio is similar to pulling or pushing the stops on an organ.

•

Musical history points out to us that:

1. Man first sang alone, producing a fundamental tone.

2. Woman then sang along an octave higher than man and, together, they sang in perfect octaves.

3. As musical history progressed into the Medieval period, organum and chant evolved, making music in perfect fourths and fifths.

4. Still later, in the Renaissance and Baroque periods, thirds were introduced.

5. In the Classical period the interval of the seventh was utilized.

6. In the Romantic period the interval of the ninth (or seconds) came into use.

7. In the Impressionistic period tenths, elevenths and thirteenths were heard.

8. In Modern music microtonal intervals are both played acoustically and electronically synthesized, etc.

In other words, the history of melody and other musical traits in western culture has directly followed the natural order of the Overtone System. The odyssey began with a solitary unison, to an octave, to fourths and fifths, to thirds, to seconds, to microtones to the inaudible.

In a *midrashic* sense, this suggests that the acoustic properties of tones are greater than just musical sounds, and are a natural, universal phenomenon emanating from a force that influences our evolution, our thinking, our musical history, and our feelings as well.

•

From these truths, the following *midrashic* observations may be made:

1. Every tone begins life as either a fundamental or a partial overtone of another fundamental.

2. Every tone is part of a larger community of allied overtones.

3. No tone is isolated or alone in the world.

4. Every tone's identity refers to the overtones that came before and follow it.

5. Overtones exist and have a direct impact upon the fundamental tone, though they might not be as prominently heard.

6. The "perfection" of an interval is found nearer to the fundamental source.

7. Even the entity that we call the fundamental or source is really part of a community of sounds. The fundamental refers to its partials for its identity, as the partials refer to the fundamental.

8. Tones continue to vibrate in the world, though humans who no longer can hear them, might assume that they have come to rest.

9. The color or quality of a tone is directly related to the other overtones that are activated and caused to vibrate along with it.

10. Some accompanying overtones are louder or more prominent than others, but all are necessary to define the quality of the fundamental.

11. If the natural series of partial tones are altered, either in progression or in amplitude (loudness), the identity and color of the fundamental will be altered as well.

12. In order to hear and identify a tone, silence must precede and follow it. Without silence punctuating its sound, a tone cannot be understood.

•

The *Midrash* of a musical tone – A meditative exercise.

1. Re-read and consider the preceding as if you are the fundamental tone, and your family, friends, and community are partial overtones in the series that is your life.

2. Re-read and consider the preceding as if God is the Fundamental, and you are a partial overtone in the great cosmic harmonic series.

3. Re-read and consider the preceding as if you are the fundamental tone, and the many aspects of your relationship with God are the partial overtones.

Conclusions

1. A tone is a multiple-system within itself. It has a pitch, color, dynamic (loudness), and an order within the sonic company it keeps.

2. When the valid life force of a tone is gratefully understood as a vibrant phenomenon, its marriage to a word takes on a much greater role. Instead of one being subservient to the other, they work synergistically to elevate the meaning of each component to greater intellectual and emotional heights. Carrying this idea a step further, when the musical relationship with a scriptural or prayer text setting is appreciated as a tripartite system made up of the text, the music, and its synergy, the levels of multiple meanings derived from this setting overwhelmingly increase both the value of the music and the significance of the text.

3. In the overtone system, as the partials resonate farther away from the fundamental, the intervals become smaller and smaller, until they can no longer be acoustically heard, but their oscillations and relationship to the fundamental tone can still be measured. This suggests that other music is still vibrating in the cosmos from before us and our music will still be vibrating after us; all interplaying in one glorious, interrelated cosmic symphony, making it easier to understand the same relationship between the body, the spirit and ultimate cosmic oneness. *Hear O Israel The Lord Our God, The Lord Is One!*

God's presence, the spirit of all those who came before us, the loss of others in our present and future life, and even our own death becomes dramatically redefined when we understand the fullest ramifications of the Overtone system. Beginnings and endings become newly understood.

All this may be gleaned from the *midrash* of a single tone.

"It is one of the commonest of mistakes to consider that the limit of our power of perception is also the limit of all there is to perceive."

—*C.W. Leadbeater*

•

Chapter 7
The *Midrash* of Time

Concentrate on three things and you will not fall into the grip of sin. Know from where you came, where you are going, and before Whom you will have to give account and reckoning.

—**Pirkei Avot**, Ethics of Our Ancestors

Judaism teaches us that the present is not only a consequence of the past, and the future the consequence of both, but to be living a full, virtuous life we are at our best when we live in all three time frames at once.

How is this science fiction possible? How does one live successfully in three simultaneous time frames? It is hard enough to be "in the moment" during the present without worrying about what has already happened and what is yet to transpire. Even if we could keep track of all the dynamics of the past, and imagine the future while we are coping with the present, are we really being "in the moment" or only going through the motions?

Torah scholar Michael Jacobs frames the challenge in this way:

Kabbalah suggests that we have two kinds of soul: the *Chaya* (animal soul) is mostly concerned with our personal needs, and the *Shechinah* or 'inner spark', which provides a unique channel to the past, future, and the world at large. Resolving conflicts that occur between these two aspects of the soul is the major challenge in our modern world. It is breaking through all the 'self-imposed' barriers of 'self interest' that enables us to begin the process (on a personal level) of 'Fixing the World ~ Tikkun Olam'.

Musicians are more at ease than others with this notion of temporal simultaneity. The best *midrashic* examples of Jewish music certainly use it as a stock in trade. Consider this illustration of three building blocks.

It can be interpreted as building blocks that may be used to create a wall of time or a development of ideas. It could also be an information highway paved with an infinite number of cobblestones like these.

Just as you would look at a portion of a cobblestone street and see this linear progression, you could also see its vertical and horizontal relationship as well.

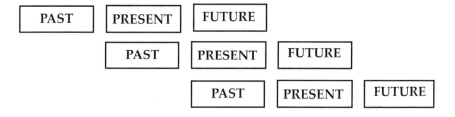

You will observe that at the same time there are at least four ways of perceiving these areas.

1. A single tense of past, present, or future

2. A dual tense of past/present, present/future, or future/past

3. A simultaneity of past/present/future

4. A continuum of past/present/future with a hole of negative space periodically between any one of them

This fourth consideration of negative space is more detailed to explain at this juncture, and I will address it more fully in the next chapter.

Music may be understood as the development of present sound ideas originating in the past that continue to evolve into the future. With this in mind, look at this cobblestone highway as a score page with each cobblestone as a measure of music. While only one measure may be under present scrutiny, two and three may also be vertically and horizontally sounding and perceived as well.

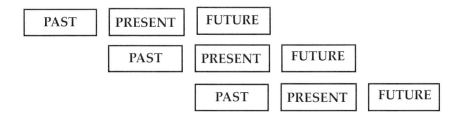

One of the many reasons for advocating the study of music as a beneficial core academic subject like language, math, or science is that it trains the eye, the ear, and the mind to think linearly, vertically, and horizontally at the same time.

When an orchestral musician plays in the present, she also is remembering the past and energizing the future in her own music. She is also listening to the music in counterpoint to her music, and the music surrounding her. In effect, the quality of her music in the present is directly dependent upon how well she can recall and employ the music of the past and initiate energies for the future as well. This is why the ability to understand the simultaneity of time is well developed and a necessary skill for trained musicians.

My composition teacher at the Eastman School of Music, Warren Benson, of blessed memory, taught that composers use this expanded simultaneous awareness as they compose each measure of their music. During this creative process they ask themselves:

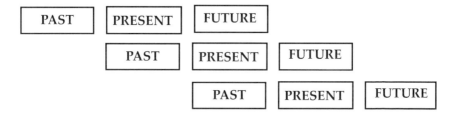

1. How can I make this present measure of music attractive and compelling?

2. How can I build in the remembrance or resonance of some aspect of a past musical idea or ideas (either melodic, rhythmic, or harmonic, etc.) into this present measure?

3. How can I create energy in this present measure that will propel the musical progress forward, evolving it into the next and future measures?

4. How can I use negative space to contrast and delineate any or all of the previous considerations?

If the composer is successful in solving each move in this three-dimensional tic-tac-toe game, then an elegant, aural logic will result. There will be an organic quality about the composed music that suggests an inevitable, natural flow that is both a convincing and organically correct path to a desired musical destination. Each measure will simultaneously succeed in three time frames

This is both the illusion and the *midrash* of time in music. The more meticulously we work to understand and effect the multiple meanings of each measure of life's music, the more inevitable and natural that meaning becomes in the larger composition of our lives. Remembering the past, making the present moment compelling, and invigorating the future creates integrity in our individual music and our collective existence.

The acclaimed actor Alan Alda, in his autobiography, writes about his well-meaning father having Alan's dead pet dog stuffed and returned home. Alda, recalling the grotesqueness of the gesture, suggests, *"Memory can be a kind of mental taxidermy, trying to hold on to the present, after it has become the past."* This is an actor's philosophy of being present in the moment as well as Alda's effort to understand and deal with the pain of his childhood.

But, to quote James Thurber's witticism:

All human beings should try to learn before they die
What they are running from, and to, and why.

More seriously, memory is not dismissed so easily in Jewish identification. I.L. Peretz, the literary and poetic voice of the *Haskalah* (19th century European Enlightenment), observed:

A people's memory is history; and as a man without a memory, so a people without a history *cannot grow wiser, better.*

•

Both Judaism and music advocate much more than just being "in the moment."

Both demand that we awake from our one-dimensional lethargy, and return to a life of heightened simultaneous awareness. In Jewish life, we give *tzedakah* (righteous charity) in memory of loved ones from the past to help individuals or institutions in the present build for their future.

In Jewish devotion, we also use these temporal dynamics. In a unified worship service, at the conclusion of many prayers, we bless God in the present, we say *Kaddish* (The magnification of God's name in the present as we honor the memory of the deceased from our past), and pray for goodness in the future. In each of these prayers, as in each measure of music, there are past, present, and future elements as well.

In the most considered Jewish music there is a simultaneous resonance of antiquity (or recollection of former times), a presence of compelling attractiveness to the music itself, and, in the best works, an innovative suggestion of where that particular music or the overall genre can progress in the future. The expectation of potentialities is a compelling consideration in Judaism.

Rabbi Leo Baeck taught in *The Pharisees:*

> Perhaps a human being does not die until he no longer sees anything but the past and the present moment.

Or, as the Hassidic master Rabbi Nachman put it:

> If you won't be better tomorrow than you were today, then what do you need tomorrow for?

The West Coast Torah scribe, visual artist, and Kabbalist Michael Jacobs, in describing the month of Elul's preparations preceding the High Holidays, observes:

> Beginning on the second day, and with the exception of Shabbatot (Sabbaths), there is a custom of sounding the Shofar (ram's horn) on each day of the month. We stand before the Creator and all of Creation and say: "This is how I have used my resources during the last year, and this is my plan for the future." The teachings of *Kabbalah Maasit* (practical kabbalah) explain that the purpose of this custom is to awaken us, to startle us into a state of remembering: Who am I? What am I doing? What should I be doing? ...And then getting on with doing it!

•

No discussion about how we use time would be complete without the thinking of the *Father of Temporal Relativity* Albert Einstein, whose Jewishness shines through when he observes:

> A hundred times a day I remind myself that my inner and outer life depend
> on the labors of other men, living and dead, and that I must exert myself in
> order to give in the measure as I have received and am still receiving.

•

Musical canons or fugues are both good examples of temporal intersection. The difference between the two is that in a fugue, an entire musical theme is stated (or mostly stated), before the next one starts. In a canon, the first one is still present when the next idea begins. Rounds (like *"Row, row, row your boat"*) are particular forms of musical imitation called perpetual canons; they have no end unless one is tacked on.

Listeners can train their ears to hear this simultaneity by listening to piano or organ recordings of J.S. Bach's canonic *Two Part Inventions* or fugues from *The Well Tempered Clavier.* I have employed this imitative technique in several of my synagogue works.

Consider recorded example #5 of a lively setting of *Oseh Shalom* from my children's Sabbath service *To Recreate the World.* It is a text found at the conclusion of the *Amidah* (the silent prayer recited while standing), composed for cantor, children's choir, adult choir, and instrumental accompaniment. The text reads:

> *Oseh shalom bim'romav, Hu ya'aseh shalom aleinu v'al kol Yisrael, v'imru: "amen."*

> May God, who creates peace in the celestial heights, create peace for us and for all Israel; and let us say, Amen.

My pre-compositional thinking usually begins with asking myself a series of stream of consciousness questions about the subject in front of me. In this case it went something like this:

> "God makes peace in the heavens and will make peace for all of us (on earth)."

1. How does God make peace on two levels — heaven and earth?

2. Is peace made simultaneously, or one after the other?

3. Can God do it alone?

4. Is it sufficient that only God makes peace?

5. Are we not God's partners in this pursuit?

6. How do humans make peace?

7. *Pirkei Avot* 1:12 - Hillel says: "Be among the disciples of Aaron, *ohev shalom v'rodef shalom*, love peace and pursue peace, by loving people, and bringing them closer to the Torah."

8. Pursuit of peace — chasing, how do we chase peace?

9. How can this setting chase (pursue) peace, bringing everyone closer to it musically?

10. Chase – canon

11. Use a canonic texture for the setting.

12. Everyone sings a different counterpoint, joining together in the end.

13. Will the children be understood if there is too much counterpoint?

14. The children are "peace" – they sing *Oseh Shalom* optimistically and steadfastly, while everyone else pursues them (the future) in counterpoint.

15. Use five metaphoric elements in *Oseh Shalom's* canonic texture:
    a. The children's unison melody (peace).
    b. The cantor's counterpoint (past tradition).
    c. The adult choir's counterpoint (present).
    d. The futuristic EWI (Electronic Wind Instrument) soprano saxophone's jazzy counterpoint (future).
    e. The rhythmic accompaniment (rooted in God's timelessness).

I began by composing a simple *Oseh Shalom* melody as a traditional chant first sung without tempo by the cantor that was then buoyantly and rhythmically echoed by the children ("*The old order changeth yielding place to new*" — Tennyson). In turn, the cantor reminds the children of tradition as he pursues peace and "chases" them, followed by the adults, then the soprano saxophone. They are all elevated in this pursuit up a modulation, go after it a bit more, and then meet as one ideal and affirm together, "Amen."

The mood needed to be joyous, as the pursuit was an affirmation of life's highest purpose. Pragmatically, this text setting, within the larger service, is heard after a long period of slow and quiet meditative service settings that now require a moment of contrasting relief. As you make yourself aware of the structure that was just outlined, see how many musical elements in this "pursuit of peace" you can listen to, identify, and follow at the same time.

Play recorded example # 5 — *Oseh Shalom* sung by Hazzan Herschel Fox.

Our senses and our intellect are capable of so much more than we usually experience. It will soon become easy for you to listen to two or three musical ideas at once.

The challenge and the joy of living then becomes the transference, development, and balanced use of this skill to hear the resonance of your past in the present, as you live a compelling life that is certain to energize and enable your future.

Oseh Shalom's setting is part of a sacred service for the Sabbath entitled *L'maaseih V'reisheet* (To Recreate the World). I was commissioned to compose it for the youth of today, who will be the

Jewish leaders of the future, by forty-three conservative, reform, and reconstructionist congregations throughout the U.S. and Canada. It was a Jewish response to the new millennium (not a celebrated event in the Jewish calendar). It was rehearsed and performed to CDs of the same standardized, pre-recorded, orchestral accompaniment played across the country simultaneously on *Shabbat Shirah* (The Sabbath of Song) in January of 2000. This innovation enabled smaller, less affluent, congregations to rehearse and perform the same composed musical sacred service with (recorded) orchestra, as the larger congregations have traditionally had access to in the past.

•

There's a charming side bar to this North American premiere. One youngster who rehearsed it for weeks in New Jersey found out, at the last moment, that she was invited to attend a *Bat Mitzvah* in another state. She was heartbroken that she would miss this historic premiere. However, when she arrived at the *Bat Mitzvah* in the new location, she found out that the host temple was performing *To Recreate the World* as well. As the pre-recorded orchestral accompaniment she had rehearsed to was standardized, she asked if she could join that choir. She did, and sang at its premiere, confidently and happily, along with over 1,300 other young choral singers across North America.

Typifying the convergence of past, present, and future, when this sacred service was given its fifth anniversary performance in January 2005, many "alumni" of the past premiere were invited to return and join the present children's choir performance. This was so successful in the true spirit of Jewish life, that it is now being planned as an ongoing tradition that will continue growing steadily into the future.

In a poem composed for *Yizkor* (the memorial remembrance) worship service, Rabbi Harold M. Schulweis of Valley Beth Shalom Temple in Los Angeles eloquently expresses the simultaneity of time.

As I look back, I know I was,
As I look at me, I know I am,
As I look beyond, I know I will be.

We are gathered at *Yizkor* to be connected in time.
Without "was" we cannot be fully in this moment.
Without "was" and "is," we cannot hold before our eyes
The foreshadowing of our future.
Hayah, Hoveh, Yih'yeh – was, is, will be.
The three tenses, when conflated, spell out the name of Divinity.

If we hold on to one tense only, we tempt idolatry.
The memories of *Yizkor* remind us we are more than what we were
And can be yet more than what we are;
A reflection of the divine unity of time.

Not where but when is Godliness?
In no space, in no place, neither above nor below,
Possible in every living moment, with every breath of life
We are created in time.
We are created in the image of three tenses,
We are mandated to remember *Hayah, Hoveh, Yih'yeh.*

Chapter 8
The *Midrash* of Space

We shape clay into a pot, but it is the emptiness inside that holds whatever we want. We work with being but non-being is what we use.

—*Lao Tzu*

The previous chapter dealing with time in music suggested that a full life is lived simultaneously in the past, present, and future. As we look at musical space, we'll explore reality from a different perspective, suggesting that what we think of as nothing is, indeed, really something.

A *midrash* on absence will then be offered teaching us we are never alone on our life's journey. There is always an invisible force in tandem with the visions, sounds, tastes, smells, and textures that we sense. This invisible but parallel *midrashic* force, once understood, is a great comfort and strength, whenever we call upon it, to gain insight and added creativity in our lives.

To begin to understand this phenomenon we must first understand the concept of *negative space*. Negative space is a visual art term that explains how shadow and the area of space around a positive shape help define that positive shape. It does not mean negative in the pejorative sense but, rather, negative in the photographic sense; that is an opposing shadow in contrast to a positive shape.

What are the implications of this simple phenomenon of light and shadow? They are profound, and when fully understood and integrated within us, capable of changing our view of life forever. Consider French poet Paul Valery's expression when he wrote:

God made the world from nothing. Sometimes, the nothingness shows through.

Is it a cynical perception or a mystical one?

The first implication of art's use of negative space is that the space between positive shapes is not absent of content. At the very least, it defines the positive shape's content and, at the very most, reveals a distinct content of its own as well. The second implication is that it is not only what we hear (or what we do) that accounts for the reality before us, but the un-heard negative space (or what we do not do) that equally delineates our reality.

On *Rosh Hashana*h (The Jewish New Year) we reflect upon both our sins of commission and our sins of omission; what we have done wrong and what remains uncorrected due to our passive inaction.

The third implication is that, in the connection and relationship of two positive shapes by negative space, it is possible to perceive a third entity. How powerful this is in understanding God's presence in our lives!

The German philosopher Franz Rosenzweig has suggested that Torah is neither wholly divine nor wholly human, but rather is a synthesis that is created in the space between God and Israel.

As a result of this observation, one definition of God might very well be what invisibly but discernibly connects and relates us to each other. Rabbi Lawrence Kushner in his anecdotal book, *God Was In This Place and I, I Did Not Know* points out that coincidences can be perceived as evidence of God's active presence in our lives.

Is it a great leap of faith to accept that what we once thought of as invisible and empty can now be infused with meaning equal in influence to the most powerful positive shapes and, in fact, defines those positive shapes in an even more powerful way?

Imagine it is your birthday or wedding or some other gala occasion, and you are seated in a regal chair in the front and center of a large grouping of your extended family posing for a family portrait.

Your grandparents, parents, siblings, husband or wife, children, aunts, uncles, and cousins are all around you smiling and happy and rejoicing. You are clearly the object of their happiness and the reason for their presence in the documentation of this grand family reunion portrait.

Fully imagine this experience. Breathe it in. Imagine the reunion that happened before the photographer snapped the photograph; imagine the celebration and stories that are shared after the picture is taken.

Now the picture is enlarged, and beautifully framed, and hung in a foyer or central spot in your home, so that each day, as you enter and exit your home you see it and reflect momentarily upon the joy of it.

On some days, you might also reflect on past or present relationships with certain individual family members. At other times, other connections might be made; but it is your family, and you are in the center of it all. The photograph is a strong positive image in your daily life.

•

Here is the second part of the exercise. In your mind, with a precise surgical scalpel, cut around your figure and the chair that you are sitting on, and remove your image totally from the picture. Color the negative space completely in black. Now stand back and ingest the gestalt of this new image.

Is it not it still a portrait of your family? Is not the family still as close? Are the dynamics between your aunts, uncles, cousins, and siblings intact? And aren't you still prominent (even in your absence) in the center of that picture, perhaps, dramatically even more so?

How have things changed? Are the relationships, perhaps, a bit more bittersweet as you reflect upon your self or members of your family portrait who must inevitably pass on? Nevertheless, aren't you still in the focus of that relationship and consideration?

•

When you understand the full extent of content and meaning that negative space carries and implies, you no longer fear the loss of a positive image (shall we call it death?), as much knowing that even though you might not be able to see that positive image, it undoubtedly exists in another form, maybe one that is even more dynamic in meaning.

How do we transfer this visual metaphor to an aural one that musicians can readily identify and use?

The obvious parallel is that there are high frequency tones, which animals can hear and humans cannot. Does this mean that the tones do not exist?

Many other animals on earth see, smell, touch, hear, and taste all kinds of stimuli that humans cannot. Do these stimuli tangibly exist in spite of our inability to perceive them? Of course they do, and their perception clearly defines the traits of the particular animal or human that perceives them!

In an adaptive musical definition negative space is the absence of any identifying musical trait, and by its conspicuous absence defines the quality and extent of other positive musical traits.

For example, it is just as much the silence between sounds that defines a rhythm as the sounds themselves. If we only had sound we would have a constant hum. The extent and the regularity of its accompanying silences define the rhythm of the positive sounds.

Composers often explore negative space as silence between sounds. They periodically use silence to create rhythms in their musical fabric. They might compose four measures of varied rhythms without pitch, as you would for a drummer, incorporating varied durations of rests as liberally as they create the sounding rhythms themselves.

When it is completed, they study it and have the option of turning it around as an opposite photographic negative, making all the silent rests into sounding rhythms and all the sounding rhythms into silent rests. Though organically conceived as negative space, the newly perceived rhythms now sound quite different. This reversal will also accompany the original nicely because one begins where the other leaves off.

It is both spiritually uplifting and comforting to understand and appreciate that these accompanying negative space rhythms were there all along, waiting to be heard and used.

•

All compositional elements are accompanied by similar negative space. Composers, in the process of creating a simple melody for a blessing or a chant, might take all the tones that are not in the melody they have created and create a contrasting "negative space" scale from them. They might then use this new scale to extend the original melody itself, by using some or all of the tones that were originally absent from it. This technique provides tonal freshness to melodic extensions, modulations, and developments.

Composers might employ the "negative space" scale to construct counterpoint, or chords to harmonize the positive tone melody. Organically allied with all the tones that are heard in a melody or in a harmony, are all those tones that are not heard, but define the ones that are heard: tonal negative space.

To reiterate, in musical terms, negative space is the absence of one identifying trait (melody, harmony, rhythm, color, etc.) that helps define its alternate presence or another trait's presence. A rhythm's rests (silences) delineate the sounding rhythm; the absented tones delineate a melody or harmony; the absented colors delineate a particular timbre; and absented stylistic devices delineate and define a particular style.

•

How is a musical idea extended and developed? Let us combine the simultaneous concepts of PAST, PRESENT, and FUTURE that we explored in the last chapter with our new understanding of negative space.

Try analyzing an event in your life by what happened before and after it. Leave a space in your mind for the event itself, as a newspaper reporter would add to a story by reporting the "color" or surrounding events. Define the impact of the central issue by understanding what went on before and after it.

For example: here is a description of a PAST:

It was just an average day, Fathers went to work, children went to school and mothers with babies spent the afternoon shopping. No one woke up a hero or set out to do extraordinary feats of bravery on that day. The only clue was from the morning weather report noting that this was, once again, 'twister season' in this sleepy, rural Texas town.

Now a description of a FUTURE:

As the twelve fatalities and seventy survivors were dug out of the once-modern supermarket in the recently built Mall, unexpected daylight overhead and a savage carnage of debris from the roof, structure, and merchandise in the aisles remained behind as a testament to the vehemence of an angry, compassionless force of nature.

As you can surmise, it is almost unnecessary to fill in the middle part. The PAST and FUTURE are so graphic that one can well imagine the violence of the tornado as it hit that supermarket and the acts of unpremeditated bravery involved in the discovery and digging out process. Indeed, any recounting of the incident without the inclusion of the PAST and the FUTURE observations would make the reporting incomplete.

•

How do composers use this negative space technique to move forward if they temporarily hit an obstacle in their writing? Simple. They temporarily skip the problematic phrase, which would be their PRESENT obstacle, and imagine the end of the process, which would be their FUTURE, and compose that concluding music. Once the bookends of PAST and FUTURE make sense, the former negative space of the PRESENT will be more clearly understood and can be composed as positive space.

Another way composers use negative space is to find the "holes" where contrasting content can be positioned. These positions sometimes happen by coincidence (divine intervention?), and sometimes the holes are pre-constructed as future compositional devices. Experience has taught me that adding well placed silences as negative spaces sets up this insertion opportunity. It is especially useful in linearly conceived music that has entrances and exits (as opposed to vertical chordal music).

In choral music, I frequently create counterpoint in Hebrew and English from the negative spaces that I have previously built in as part of the initial exposition.

•

Play recorded example #6 *Make Me A Sanctuary,* **sung by Cantor Jay Frailich, the first of three choral settings from** *The Renewal Suite.*

The theme of the text is God's mandate to create something that does not exist for a Deity that exists everywhere, at all times (even when we do not perceive God's presence).

In its musical construction, a linguistic *midrash* employing Hebrew, contrasting English, and a timbral contrast between the solo cantor and the choir uses principles of negative space. Note the *staccato* (Italian: short and separated) choral articulations that also provide "air" (negative space) in between the sung vowels.

Here is the text:

Make Me A Sanctuary Exodus 25:8,9 Genesis 1 (adapted by M.I.)

Choir—Make Me a Sanctuary, build Me a House of God

Cantor – *V'asu li Mikdash, v'shachanti b'tocham*

Choir – And let them make Me a Sanctuary that I may live among them.

Cantor – *K'chol asher ani mareh ot'cha k'eit tavnit haMishkan*

Choir—Make Me a sanctuary that I may live among you according to all that I show you after the pattern of the Tabernacle.

Cantor—*Ayaar Elohim et kol asher asah v'hinei tov m'od.*

Choir—God saw everything that was made and, behold, it was very good.

As you listen, note where English and Hebrew texts begin and end and their relationship to other voices. Understanding negative space and its potential created those opportunities for entrances and exits of the two languages.

Judaism teaches us that absence may mean the non-being of something but not everything. Very often when "We let go, we let God in"facilitating all things. There is a term in *Kabbalah* (Jewish mysticism) that nicely explains negative space from a theological point of view. The term is *tsimtsum*. In the beginning, before creation, God was everywhere. The Holy Presence had to "implode" to create space for the universe. *Tsimtsum* is the act of that withdrawal and contraction into an elemental concentration of energy.

As parents we often feel that we have to micromanage every part of our children's lives. Psychologically, the *midrash* of *tsimtsum* teaches us that when we temporarily "implode" (or back off), enabling our creations to find their own "space" (as God enables humanity to do), our creations find their own worth or Godliness because first, now, and always there is only God.

This *midrash* of absence reminds us that we are never isolated or alone, and that our work on earth must be to perceive and value negative space, all the latent energy it implies, and then, intelligently and compassionately, gather that energy in the act of transforming, delineating, and creating positive existence..

•

In recorded example #7, *They Are Children*, from a Synagogue dramatic work for *Shavuot* entitled *A Covenant of Wonder*, Jerry Whitman, as Moses, sings to God of his impatience with the Children of Israel. While we do not hear a worded response from God, in that negative space the repetition of an instrumental "cloud" suggests God's omnipresence and guidance in the discussion. The stage direction suggests that at these moments "Moses listens." As you listen, imagine what God is saying and fill in that negative space with your own empathy and creativity. This is how active listening realizes the music's fullest meaning.

Play recorded example #7 *They Are Children*, sung by Jerry Whitman.

Using the analogy of a cobblestone street from the previous chapter, negative spaces are those gaps that define the stones of time and space in music, and in all the thoughtful arts.

In a visual, *midrashic* fashion, the optical illusion or "Impossible Art" below, created by the Swedish artist Oscar Reutersvard during the 1930's, graphically sums up this chapter's discussion. The Jewish *midrashic* interpretation is my own.

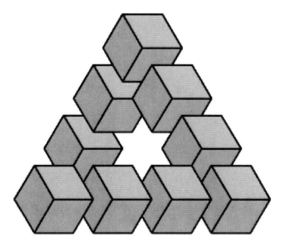

At the heart of it is a *Magen David* (A Star of David), representing the Jewish spirit in the center of the most durable geometric shape—a triangle.

Yet, it is made from negative space, and *tsimtsum*—God's imploded presence. (Is it real or is it an illusion?). Surrounded by tenuously held together detached entities (as quantum physics and Kabbalah tell us we all are), its singular shape, though born in wonder, gives focus, unity, and hope to a world moving in ambiguous and conflicting directions. The image, a string theory visual metaphor, is also a beautiful visual example of the *midrash* of space.

Chapter 9
The *Midrash* of Separation

Blessed are You, Ruler of the Universe, who distinguishes between the sacred and the secular, between light and dark, between Israel and the nations, between the seventh day and the six days of labor. Blessed are You, who distinguishes between the sacred and the secular. — Final Havdalah Blessing

In defining one aspect of the negative space discussed in the previous chapter, Hillel is quite clear in his advocacy of the separation of a spiritual life from a materialistic, hedonistic existence, when he writes in Avot 2:7:

> The more flesh the more worms, the more property the more worry, the more wives the more witchcraft, the more maids the more lewdness, the more menservants the more theft; the more Torah the more life, the more study the more wisdom, the more counsel the more understanding, the more charity the more well being.

"Things" bring excess and trouble, while understanding and charity facilitate glimpses of paradise on earth.

But how do composers use the *midrash* of separation to create music out of apparent nothingness?

We can learn much about the creative process by reading of the creation of the world in the beginning chapter of Genesis. The primary paradoxical lessons of creation are that nothing comes from nothing, and not everything is equal and to be lumped together as a homogeneity. At the outset, components have to be identified, separated, divided, classified, and evaluated, just as a painter names, selects, and separates his colors on a palette before beginning to paint. In fact, most of the world's creation is achieved through separation. Here are just the first two days:

1. In the beginning God created the heaven and the earth.

2. And the earth was without form, and void; and darkness was upon the face of the deep. And the Spirit of God moved upon the face of the waters.

3. And God said, let there be light: and there was light.

4. And God saw the light, that it was good: and God divided the light from the darkness.

5. And God called the light Day, and the darkness He called Night. And the evening and the morning were the first day.

6. And God said, Let there be a firmament in the midst of the waters, and let it divide the waters from the waters.

7. And God made the firmament, and divided the waters, which were under the firmament from the waters, which were above the firmament: and it was so.

8. And God called the firmament Heaven. And the evening and the morning were the second day.

Creation continues through the next four days by dividing, gathering one entity from another, and separating components, by giving them names and distinct identities.

Division, separation, classification, and hierarchy are also central facets of a combined discipline in musical creation and living as a Jew, both in one's personal life and communal interaction. Humorously, here is what Samuel Cohon, Rabbi of Temple Emanu-El, in Tucson, Arizona, writes about separation in his Temple's bulletin.

> "My father and I have an old story we trot out now and then. We say that when I was studying to be a cantor I asked him, "How do you handle the Temple 's board of directors?" And he answered, "How do I handle the board of directors? Like this: "We have an agreement. I don't come to their meetings, and they don't go to my services...."

> But the notion that there is an essential wall of separation between the praying, studying, and teaching parts of a temple and the business end of the enterprise is a well-established tradition. And the fact of the matter is that we do the same things in our own daily lives. Most of us create a kind of wall of separation between our Jewish life -- which exists at temple, or perhaps on Friday nights and holidays at home -- and our "regular life." We have a very limited notion about how much Judaism is supposed to be allowed to influence our everyday lives and the decisions we make that are of real importance to us.

> Mostly this is a simple question of choosing to limit the ways in which we allow our religious life to influence our daily actions. For example, how often do you ask yourself if an activity you are about to engage in is appropriate or seemly for a Jew? How often do you consider if the way in which you are going to use your time increases holiness in your life, or seeks to improve the world? Sometimes the questions are simpler, and more mundane, but no less Jewish or important: What percentage of your income do you choose to give to tzedakah? What was the last Jewish class you took? When was the last time you really prayed?"

Jewish ritual underlines separation in its fundamental tenets of *kashrut* (separating certain animals as kosher, separating dairy from meat, separating utensils, separating the order of ingestion, etc.), *Shatnes* (separating linen from wool in clothing), sexual activity (times to separate and times to engage), and, of course, *Shabbat* and holiday activities. In fact, the chanting of *Havdalah* (the ritual of separating the holy from the mundane) concludes every Sabbath day. Ultimately, the Hebrew word for holiness itself is *kadosh*, which can also be interpreted as separate and apart.

•

How is separation achieved in music? Is there really a sacred music that is separate from the mundane?

While it would be foolish to ascribe any one musical style or "sound" with a sense of holiness over another style, there are some guidelines for creating music that distances us from the secular experience and enables us to transcend those mundane concerns for a moment or two and leave them at the synagogue door, while we aspire to accessing a higher consciousness.

In the negative space of the secular din that surrounds us, music of holiness can be found. To find this negative space one only has to analyze and characterize the mindless music of television commercials, computer jingles, the incessant use of iPods, cell phone rings, call waiting, "elevator music," and all the other mini-formats whose job it is to distract us from thinking and feeling, and then identify the music that is not found in these moments. Some guidelines include:

1. **Sacred music should be music that is thoughtfully listened to and considered, not just heard, felt, and dismissed.**

This pertains to each of its musical elements as well. For example, repetitious rhythms turn off our cognitive brains and critical listening faculties. While other religions might encourage "trance music," Jewish music asks us to think and feel while we listen in a balanced experience. Melodies that too strongly recall secular experiences diminish holiness and discount their appropriateness. Tempos that are too fast do not give us adequate time to make meanings. Instrumental colors (like saxophones, electric guitars and basses, and conga drums), usually associated with non-religious experiences, distract us from a sense of dedicated occasion, and uniqueness. Sacred music requires separation.

One of the seminal works burned by the Nazis was Austrian Author Franz Werfel's 1931 book *Realism and Inwardness*. In it he writes:

> *Without inwardness there can be no external world, and without imagination there can be no reality.*

Those who advocate making synagogue music sound interchangeable with what is heard outside of the synagogue,or the same as *Top Ten* popular programming, have simply missed the wisdom of separation and elevation in the worship experience.

2. Sacred music that sets words should help us connect with those words and digest their import more clearly.

Sensitive settings that show care for stressing the correct syllables of the words in the text should be employed; music should be chosen that serves the text rather than vice-versa; and an observable *midrash* of the text should be a component part of that music.

3. If the music is wordless, then it should bring us to a quiet reverence or a not-so-quiet ecstasy that we could not attain outside of the synagogue.

There should be a distinctive, stylistic purity to the experience with a timelessness that defies momentary, *au courant* "hipness."

A useful rule of thumb might be to ask, "Am I hearing 'cross-over' music imposed upon a sacred occasion, or is it music that is not usually or frequently heard outside the synagogue, and was created specifically for this worship and spirituality?"

An ancillary question might be, "Does the timeliness of the music cloud the classic timelessness of the spiritual connection?"

Of course, with all generalizations, balance and perspective need to temper absolutes. I have used "secular" rhythms and harmonies in framing melodies, but I try never to confuse the totality of what I hear outside of the synagogue with what I hope to create or hear inside of it.

When I was invited by my life-long friend Rabbi Stephen Pearce to create a new work for the Congregation Emanu-El of San Francisco's 150th anniversary, I was honored to compose a complete *Havdalah* service, framed by an opening *nigun* (meditative song without words) with three new poetic interpolations authored by Rabbi Pearce. These evocative poems, *Sweet Vapors Ascend*, *Cinnamon Bay and Cloves*, and *Night's Blackness*, describe the sensual and mystical qualities of the wine, the spices, and the flame associated with the ritual.

The poetic interpolations, set in a contrasting, abstract musical language, separate the more accessible *Havdalah* tune (*Havdalah* means separation), and momentarily access a transcendent world of meaning apart from the weekly concluding ritual of farewell for the Sabbath. As Cantor Roslyn Barak has done so artfully on this companion recording, ephemeral, evanescent word pictures are created that elevate the texture and meaning of each *Havdalah* symbol.

•

Let me take you through this distinctive *Havdalah Suite* in recorded example #8 to demonstrate how the idea of separation (and its negative space – a sense of return) influences and colors the work's elements, thereby creating a *midrash*.

The work begins with a *nigun* (a wordless song presented as the first musical example in Chapter 1) that creates a separation between the incipient silence of the dark and the first text of the ritual.

1. *Nigun* (Wordless Song) For Sabbath's Farewell

The abstraction of the preparatory *nigun* gives way to a set text chanted in a traditional *nusach* (prayer scale).

Play example #8 *Havdalah Suite* sung by Cantor Roslyn Barak

2. Hinei Eil Y'shuati – Havdalah, Blessing Over Wine

Liturgy - *Hinei Eil y'shuati evtach v'lo efchad ki ozi v'zimrat yah Adonai vay'hi li l'shuah. Ush'avtem mayim b'sason mimainei hayishuah L'Adoni hay'shuah al amcha virchatecha selah.*

Adonai ts'vaot imanu, misgav lanu Elohei Yaakov selah. Lay'hudim hay'tah orah v'simcha v'sason vikar; kein tih'yeh lanu. Kos y'shuot esah uv'sheim Adonai ekrah.

A more identifiably modern melody separates us from the *nusach* as we make the *Havdalah's* meaning our own in a more idiomatic expression.

(Isaacson lyric) - Havdalah making a difference in our world and in our own hearts, Havdalah blessing the difference as the light of Shabbat departs.

Back to the liturgy.

Liturgy - *Baruch Atah Adonai, Eloheinu, Melech Haolam, borei p'ri hagafen.*

Another separate and differentiated plane of understanding is approached through modern poetry that is set in a contrasting musical vocabulary from the previous settings.

3.   Pearce - Sweet Vapors Ascend

Sweet vapors ascend slaking longings for distant days of salvation's cup filled from redemption's wells. Drink deeply. A lingering bouquet calls *l'chaim* from a distant place: Havdalah's elixir raises spirits crestfallen. Chayei olam notah b'tocheinu. Thank You, O God, for Shabbat's foretaste of eternity as the last of fading light vanishes.

We return to the melody of the first blessing.

4.   Isaacson - *Havdalah* – Blessing Over Spices

Havdalah, the wisdom of differing commonplace from holiness. Let us recall the spices of Eden as the light of Shabbat comes to rest.

Liturgy - *Baruch atah Adonai, Eloheinu melech haolam borei minei b'samim.*

We return to Rabbi Pearce's poetry.

5.   Pearce - **Fragrant Spices**

Cinnamon, bay and clove ascend from wild flowered meadow and gently flowing watercourses, awakening from winter's grasp. Pungent woodland bark, forest fragrances, cedar's scent arise recalling Eden. If only every day were Eden, if only every day were spring, I would hear a sweet scented melody of *b'samim* singing the heart's song.

We return once again to the familiar melody of the first blessing.

6. **Isaacson** - *Havdalah* – Blessing over the Flame

> Havdalah even in darkness, Havdalah our vision sustains a peaceful world of joy and gladness as the memory of Shabbat remains.

Liturgy - *Baruch atah Adonai, Eloheinu melech haolam borei m'orei ha-eish.*

The third of Rabbi Pearce's poems is set.

7. **Pearce** - Sacred Fire

> Night's blackness overtakes light's last graying rays as delicate, white woven filaments and waxen beads unite; light and darkness collide. Creation's mystery, revelation's promise, redemption's dawn under a vast sky where unnumbered descendents appear in brilliance. We, the stars of heaven, the sands of the seashore, and the sacred fire of light are one.

We once again separate from the symbols and return to the melody of the opening nigun that now has become the conveyance of the traditional text about differentiating the holy from the common place.

8. *Liturgy* - *Hamavdil*

> *Hamavdil bein kodesh l'chol, bein or l'choshech, bein yisrael l'amim, bein yom hash'vi-i, l'sheishet y'mei ha-ma-a-seh. Baruch atah Adonai, hamavdil bein kodesh l'chol.*

We proceed to yet another time and space and musical separation of mood, rhythm, and melody in the setting of the traditional folk text of Elijah the Prophet, who will herald the Messiah's return.

9. **Folk**- *Eliyahu Hanavi*

Eliyahu Hanavi, Eliyahu Hatishbi, Eliyahu Hagiladi. Bimheirah b'yameinu yavoh eileinu im mashiach ben David.

A final separation and return to the *Havdalah* melody (and a brief quote of the *Eliyahu Hanavi* tune) to begin the week with an optimistic energy.

10. **Isaacson** - *Shavuah Tov*

Shavuah Tov, a good week repairing, Shavuah Tov, our world and our soul; Shavuah Tov, a week of returning again when Shabbat makes us whole. A week for repairing, a week for renewing, a week for improving our world. Shavuah Tov, a good week, a week of peace, Shavuah Tov.

This *Havdalah* interpretation is founded on the principles of separation (and return) in word and wordless settings, musical language, instrumentation, mood, structure, and vocabulary.

In utilizing this doctrine of separation within its movements, and in the larger totality, a specific, unique composition is created that could only be meant for this specific moment.

This is the *midrash* of the music. While we return each week to the Sabbath, we separate ourselves in our weekly rhythms and tempo of communication and even modify our vocabulary. We nurture the poetic aspect of our lives and reconnect with our tradition.

Our separation from one set of practices enables us to return to another set reserved for the Sabbath. This *Havdalah* musical setting comments, offering a *midrash,* on the separation of the sacred from the secular, by separating the poetic from the simple, and tradition from innovation. It creates levels of a distinctive musical existence beyond the words that refresh our understanding of what we have left behind us and to what we are about to return.

Chapter 10
The *Midrash* of Drama

In the dark of the theatre we remember ourselves. And we know we are not average men and that Madison Avenue shall not sell us that we are. Our nerves signal us again, as via Telstar, directly across the ocean of the orchestra pit, straight to the pit of our stomachs with the pitiless speed of feeling which, if not faster, is more revealing than light.

—Sidney Michaels, Preface to his play Dylan

The two real challenges to satisfying worship and congregational growth in synagogues today and, indeed, consistent communal spiritual beliefs, are our philosophical notions about individualism and relativism. If the individual is valued over the group, why bother to pray together? And if your truth is as relatively correct as mine, or any other, why bother to collectively share these emphasizing one over another?

The answer, of course, is that there is an inherent drama being played out when we express our longings and devotion in the company of others, as well as witness their petitions, and search for a meaningful nexus with God. The quality of that drama, as a means, is as important as the prayer itself in making that connection. This is the power of a well-conceived, dramatic congregational service.

In creating a successful congregational experience, ideas must be presented in a convincing way to replace individualism and relativism with larger-than-life, compelling sights and sounds that celebrate the bigger picture of who we are, what we believe to be good and true, and what we are capable of feeling and becoming as a Godly people. Sacred music, when presented majestically and persuasively, gives our worship and life-cycle celebrations the "importance," "size," and, ultimately, focus, that they require. As Rabbi Abraham Isaac Kook proposed:

> Contemplate the wonders of creation, the Divine dimension of their being, not as a dim configuration that is presented to you from a distance, but as the reality in which you live.

The best sacred music contains a sense of heightened drama. In synagogue music, a cantor pleading to God on behalf of his people communicates great urgency, even if that chant is inner directed in almost a whisper. In all sacred spaces, there is an emotionally convincing, synergistic energy that great choral music, or congregational singing, brings to the task of spiritual elevation or appeal. The very nature of petition is dramatic need. Connecting to the source of a benevolent God (perhaps the Godliness within each of us), who is omnipresent and wishes us to succeed in living a good life, is best achieved in focused, dramatic fashion.

If we consider the synagogue or temple not as a museum of an ancient religion, or as a diversionary summer campfire, but as a *Theatre of the Spirit*, then fresh innovative ways of communicating Judaism's highest goals can be attained through sacred music with dramatic values.

Why is it important to find drama in our religious worship music? Aren't traditions, ethical texts, and observance of laws enough to guide us on the right path without the extra aura of drama and theatricality wrapped up in mystical worship services?

Empirical observation and history teach us that human beings most effectively access and individually tend to their intimate inner longings and hopes by becoming part of worship communities. These congregations seek ongoing relationships with God through outward involvement in larger-than-life communal religious worship.

The design of the holy temples, the architecture and the inner appointments of the great Christian cathedrals, the paintings of the Sistine Chapel, the Chagall windows in the Hadassah Hospital chapel, the huge Masses of Palestrina, Bach, Mozart, Beethoven, Berlioz, and the Requiems of Brahms and Verdi, and the Bloch Sacred Service, all huge, artistic works in the name of God, were created to reinforce artistically and dramatically our sense of spiritual grandeur.

•

How impoverished our religious lives would be without this desire to portray God's influence upon us in the grandest, most emotionally profound fashion! After all, who wants to invest one's devotion and hopes in a puny God?

What is drama? Like *aggadic midrash*, it is vivid storytelling, usually using forms of struggle or conflict, to reach an ultimately larger-than-life understanding and appreciation of the truth about what is good, just, and right in the world. What is religion? It is a way of learning and practicing what is good, just, and right by means of vivid storytelling in its highest biblical refinement (usually using forms of struggle or conflict), and submitting to a larger-than-life conception of a higher power.

The two seem to be inextricably paired. Greek drama began with the history of conversations between the gods. What could be more dramatic than God's conversations with Moses and the biblical recounting of the historic Exodus from Egypt or the parting of the Sea of Reeds?

The essential components of these two interrelated areas are: a larger than life conception; vivid story telling; conflict; and rooting for the good to be rewarded and the evil punished.

From these ideas we can discern seven dramatic *midot* principles which, when applied, will increase our *midrashic* appreciation of musical settings of narratives (all art is storytelling) and make their message all the more compelling. Employing these seven principles in our critical assessment will help us improve the quality of our sacred music programming.

Seven Dramatic Principles in Sacred Music

1.   Value music that creates a larger than life conception.

In Genesis, God creates the world in six days, and on the seventh day God rests. This teaches us that we are capable of recreating our own world each week for the better, and that setting time off for rest, prayer, and meditation each week is good for us in the short term and, ultimately, an economical, productive strategy in the larger picture as well.

Would this same lesson be taught to us as effectively if the Bible had reported: "God created the world in an evolutionary manner over millions of years with interims of upheaval alternating with periods of relative stasis?"

No, of course not! It is the incredibly mythic finiteness of the seven days and the miraculous surge of creation within it that makes God all the more of a deity and encourages us to be humble worshippers.

In another Genesis story, Cain murders Abel to illustrate that we must all be responsible for keeping and caring for our brothers (and sisters), or else pay the heavy price of losing favor with God.

Would the same lesson be taught to us if Cain forgot to send Abel a birthday card, or merely had a sibling quarrel with him? No, it is the larger-than-life dramatic shock of murder, which viciously demands that this precept of being "my brother's keeper" be understood in the most primitive, primal way.

So it is with sacred music. A composer devises a way to rivet our attention to the subject at hand through a larger-than-life gesture. It might be as simple as a wide melodic interval sung fortissimo, an unconventional harmonic setting of a key word in the text, the use of an instrument normally not employed in the service, the provocative juxtaposition of English and Hebrew texts, or a musical attitude that seems, at first, irreverent of the text, but then justifies itself. All these can serve as larger-than-life devices to call attention to the subject at hand.

I shall never forget the congregational impact of Lawrence Goldberg's operatic setting of the *Sacrifice of Isaac,* which I had the privilege to stage and conduct at its premiere. At the moment when God's angel traditionally stays Abraham's hand and prevents the killing of his beloved son, Isaac, the composer had Abraham plunge the knife deeply and fully into his son: fulfilling God's commandment through the inconceivable, macabre completion of the act.

The congregation audibly gasped at what they had just seen and heard. There was a moment of bleak silence as they absorbed this unthinkable reality. Then the Angel of God invoked the blessing found in the daily *Amidah* (prayer recited silently while standing), *"Blessed are You, O Lord, Ruler of the Universe who brings back to life the dead,"* and Isaac slowly rose, and rejoined his father in finding the lamb in the thickets for the conclusion.

This dramatic setting is a wonderful example of a larger-than-life conception. It needn't be as extreme in every composition, but music that pays attention to this principle will have a congregation paying attention to this music.

One can only wonder what this generation's constant menu of meagerly conceived and performed music, accompanied by guitar, will do to their concept of God. While Martin Buber, in his *I - Thou* philosophy, advocated an intimacy with our Creator, his use of the formal *"Thou"* also balanced it with a larger-than-life contrasting aspect of divinity. Both are necessary for balance.

2. Value music that presents a fresh point of view.

Concomitant to finding "the holes in the catalog" (unfulfilled needs), composers, cantors, and congregations should always be searching for a point of view that offers a fresh, un-clichéd perspective or insight. This does not always mean that a new setting is better. Very often, returning to an older, classic setting of a text will sound fresher than more of the same.

After surveying the literature, to learn what has and has not been done, a composer asks, "What dramatic elements have not been or seldom been explored in relation to this subject?" What approach to this subject reflects a historical "knowingness," a reflection of present values, style, vocabulary, and might even suggest future alternatives all at the same time? Then the composer dares to be different.

For example, at Rosh Hashanah services, I was always a little disappointed by the blandness of the *shofar* service at my temple. The *shofar* (Ram's horn) is a dramatically exotic, historical instrument that has at least three profound meanings to it during the larger service, but is rather routinely blown and put away during closely scheduled, time-oriented, modern services. The biggest concern and thrill when I was growing up seemed to be counting how long the *Baal Shofar* (the shofar blower) could hold the concluding *t'kiah g'dolah* (the final great, long blast*)*.

After researching the literature, I discovered that no one had ever composed a *shofar* service for brass quintet, choir and, of course, *shofar* with poetic interpolations. I immediately set out to do it.

I studied the three aspects of the *shofar's* meaning: *malchuyot*, (the coronation of God as our supreme monarch), *zichronot* (memories of God's moral order), and *shofrot* (the ultimate call for liberation and the welcoming of the Messianic Age). New inspiration flooded my mind like morning light from an open window. I quickly found poems and readings which brought these meanings closer to home for the congregation, and composed interpolated movements for the brass quintet that would also amplify the drama inherent in the *shofar's* three calls.

The result is a *shofar* service called *Kol T'ruah*. It answered a need that I personally felt and found a fresh way of going about fulfilling. The poetic interpolations give the soloists and choir something special to do with brass quintet. The overall dramatic effect is both ancient and strikingly new.

When listening to a text or a musical setting in any service, we must think for a moment. Asking ourselves: What's already been done? How has it been done? Do these treatments satisfy our aesthetic values, and connect us to the subject? If they leave us wanting, then it's our turn and creative opportunity to repair this deficiency by asking for something new.

3. Have a clear understanding of the premise and conventions of a dramatic work in its first moments.

In an hour-long work, we will concentrate for about three to five minutes until we convince ourselves that we understand what's going on, what the piece is about, and what the rules or conventions of this particular musical activity are. After that, without the proper orientation, we get restless, confused, and increasingly hostile (or worse – bored). In the usual duration of a sacred work, about three minutes, we have only fifteen seconds or so to understand the premise and engage our interest.

How can a composition establish anything in fifteen seconds? Consider Beethoven's first ten measures of the *Fifth Symphony*, beginning with, "Da Da Da Daaaa."

The entire orchestra begins, ferociously, letting us know the piece will move with symphonic passion around the interval of a descending major third. It will be worked over and over, as only Beethoven can do, and by the fifth and sixth measures we understand the gymnastic plan in the orchestration as well. We know the rules of that piece instantly and in less than fifteen seconds are completely engrossed by its subject.

Knowing or not knowing the rules of a piece of music as it is initially unfolds is analogous to watching a baseball game without knowing what strikes, balls, ground rule doubles, and all the rest are about. It becomes quite a different experience with a much lower appreciation quotient.

Active listeners keep asking themselves: What is the prevailing mood? What is the subject, and what is the theme? Has it a subtext? Is there a dramatic conflict? What is its attitude toward the subject, and what is the level of sophistication of the larger work? Is it clearly suggested in the opening? Does the introduction foreshadow and reflect what will follow and develop? Does it take too long to get to the point? In other words, is the opening scene in the first reel compelling enough for us to stay glued for the entire movie?

Immediate identification with the piece and letting the audience know what it is initially about are fundamental theatre concepts that cross over into the arena of sacred music as well.

In Stephen Sondheim's account of the making of *A Funny Thing Happened On The Way To The Forum,* based on an obscure Roman comic spectacle with many turns in the plot, he admitted that the opening never seemed initially to grab the audience, until a new opening number, *Comedy Tonight,* was added. *Comedy Tonight* lyrically tells the audience exactly who the main characters are, what their goals are during the course of the show, exactly who the good guys and the bad guys are, and who the audience should root for; all in one opening song.

The same concept is used in *Tradition,* the opening number of *Fiddler on the Roof.* Tevye, his wife and daughters, and the townspeople are all introduced. You know Tevye's story will involve a conflict between marrying off his daughters and the emotional tether of his Jewish traditions.

In the concert hall, consider Mozart's mysterious trombone chordal opening to the *Magic Flute, o*r Bernstein's finger snapping opening to *West Side Story,* or Debussy's moody opening to *La Mer,* or Stravinsky's pagan solo bassoon in the *Rite of Spring:* all wonderful examples of setting up the premise immediately and grabbing our attention as listeners.

It needn't be complicated or take long. (In fact, if it takes too long the composer has not succeeded.) But the musical gesture and initial information must structure and whet our expectations, immediately and effectively, or we will simply lose attention.

Using computer parlance, the efficacy of setting up the premise clearly gives us time to retrieve from our brains files which contain the memories of similar types of stories that we have previously seen, heard, or experienced.

We then use this retrieved information to analyze, compare, and comment upon the data that we are about to experience. If this data is not retrieved and available when the new material is being input, the brain has no context in which to process it.

The reason we know a chair is a chair is because we compare it with our stored data of what a chair looks like, functions as, and the possible variations in its form. If we didn't have data to compare, half the present experience would be devoted to defining that chair. Greater meanings would be impeded and postponed, causing us to uncomfortably fall behind in the narrative's progress.

When the premise is delineated quickly and engagingly at the very outset, we are given an opportunity to call up established data files and prepare intelligently for the new story. This comforts us and enables the composer or storyteller to make friends with the audience, assuring us that when we are most vulnerable, at the beginning of a new experience, that our imminent journey has been thoughtfully planned for our maximum enjoyment.

4. Value music that has built-in reminders, helping us to remember what has been set out to be important.

Less experienced composers sometimes worry that a restatement of a theme or any other varied reiteration for that matter may be too redundant: "I've said that already, am I repeating myself too often?" To a certain extent the composer is correctly concerned.

Constant repetition is dull and uncreative. However, intelligently varied and precisely calculated repetitions at certain key structural moments are both desirable, and absolutely necessary.

It is fascinating, when studying an opera or a musical, to see how often a melody or a melodic fragment is repeated during the course of an evening's performance. First, we might hear it in the overture. Then, it is stated fully. Then,we might hear it repeated again and again in the underscore. Then, it is referred to in the entr'acte. Then, it is reprised and, finally, heard once more in the exit music. Does anyone wonder why we hum and remember it as we walk out of the theatre? Have you ever heard anyone complain that a melody was repeated too many times? The contrast between the audience's perception of the melody and the composer's perception is quite different. While a composer lives months and months with a work during its creation, laboring over the same theme for countless hours to the point of distraction, we, the audience, are hearing the whole work for the very first time!

Repetition and re-emphasis of key structural elements are essential in weaving patterns into an aural tapestry that is to be clearly perceived. While endless repetition is boring, it is almost impossible to be too intelligently reminiscent in music.

Recurring aural signposts direct the way to our understanding of the music and provide a familiar landscape.

One reason that abstract serial music cannot easily be recalled is that exact repetition of the original row is scarce in this form. If we can't recall it after two or even three hearings, we won't ever remember it and attentively recognize it as we follow its developmental journey.

No matter how ingenious a compositional invention or variation is, if an audience can't readily recall it and use the theme or motif as a key to understanding larger compositional issues, the work has failed to communicate its idea effectively.

In the Bloch *Avodas Hakodesh* (Sacred Service) the motif, "Sol la do si la sol" keeps varying and repeating throughout, adding a wonderful cohesiveness and purity of focus to the music. We appreciate its repetition. It points us to the author's larger message and gives us a precious tool for understanding the more complex features of the work.

5. Value music whose subject is presented attractively, so that we can root for its success.

First, a listener ascertains what a composition will be about, and the main melodic, harmonic, rhythmic, timbral, or structural idea that will serve as the focus, or protagonist, of the musical drama. The idea goes on to encounter conflict, struggles to emerge victorious, and develop and grow creatively.

We anticipate engaging ancillary ideas that attract us and periodically return as repetitions. In this format these landmarks serve as "progress reports," leading us to the final heroic climax in which the compositional idea's growth, maturity, and versatility will be certified and finalized in a life-affirming cadence.

We hope for an empathy with the main musical idea, an ongoing identification that elevates and validates the time and concentration we have attentively devoted to active listening.

Have you ever gone to a movie or a play that features an antihero? An antihero is a person or group who, through unattractive behavior, anti-social values or destructive attitudes, advocates just the opposite of what a hero should stand for. Hopefully, we always wait to see if these antiheroes will be redeemed at the end or, somehow, through acquired clarity, find the direction home again. We yearn for the good to be triumphant.

When this does not occur, we usually leave the experience more than a bit frustrated by the shallowness and meaninglessness of it all. There are some writers, filmmakers, and composers today who don't find the need to have good triumph over evil, or virtue rewarded. They justify the attention they have paid to the antiheroic subject's outrageous behavior as "a sign of our times," or "a slice of life." Candidly, if I want a slice of life, I do not need to go to the theatre or the movies, or find it in the concert hall. Each morning I read the paper and view the news on TV, and learn of atrocities in human relations that I never dreamed could come about.

There is nothing extraordinary about people behaving poorly to each other and themselves. They do it all the time. There seems to be plethora of anti-heros in our everyday reality and in the media's desire to dig deep enough to reveal all the flaws of any heroic contender.

The frustration of many younger artists may be stated as: "How can I advocate an art that roots for the good guys when there are none presented to me?" The answer is that art provides the greatest opportunity for elevation of our mind and heart. Artists are vitally necessary in our lives to promote those epiphanies. Sacred music, in particular, encourages us to root for the quintessential "good guy."

Whether it is a memorable poetic text or a haunting melody, a catchy rhythm or a colorful orchestration, the main idea has to be appealing to the listener. We want to root for its development, return, and resolution.

All music need not be heroic to be attractive. However, if it is clever but emotionally dry, intricate but distant, simple but crassly common, or direct but only one dimensional, it will make it more challenging for us to make friends with the main idea and stalwartly follow it on its musical odyssey.

Regretfully, we have all been to concerts to hear music that is respected but not loved. We usually exit these experiences unsatisfied, as if having had a nourishing but tasteless meal. There are also moments when the music is so engagingly attractive, so heroic, infused with so much belief, that we sing and pray with delight.

Then there is also the music that is so intent on being "hip" and stylistically cutting edge that, in its one-dimensional fixation, it forgets to communicate timeless ideas in a timeless voice.

Skillful composers may freely season their music with the harshest dissonance, outrageous orchestration, or any and all avant-garde techniques. However, they don't neglect to hang them on the torso of inherently likable musical ideas. When we experience wild anarchy, it is good to be assured that, in the end, a satisfying compositional redemption will be at hand. It is not enough to respect the intellect and craft of music. It must also win us over emotionally in a multi-dimensional way.

This is why tonal music ultimately cadences on a coming home tonic chord, and even dissonant works often find their repose in perfect unisons, fifths or octaves. They represent a necessary closure and a sense of completion.

When we wrestled with a definition for Jewish music, it was suggested that the "Jewishness" had less to do with the composer's ethnicity or the sound of the actual music than with the quality of *drash*, or comment upon the aspect of Judaism being addressed by the music. The final two principles call attention to how we can understand and specifically access this *midrashic* commentary in Jewish music.

6. Understand how a sub-text is revealed and reinforced in musical ways.

What is a subtext? A subtext is not to be confused with a subplot, which is a secondary story usually found in narratives. Using the more advanced *Pardes* levels, a subtext is a deeper, primal meaning or dramatic motivation found by delving into a seemingly simple text and allowing its surface subject to transport our attention to its meatier, more profound message.

For example, the *Kol Nidre* text, which we recite on the evening before *Yom Kippur* (the Day of Atonement), is not really a prayer at all, but a legal formula nullifying and canceling all vows, not between two human beings, but only those made between a person and God.

The text stems from Gaonic times (760 CE). Its inclusion in the liturgy was disputed by the rabbis, who feared that it would fuel anti-Semitic propaganda that Jews could not be trusted to keep their promises.

This historical argument was put aside in the Diaspora (especially after the expulsion from Spain in 1492), when Jews had to renounce their Jewish identity and convert to Catholicism to stay alive. Once a year these Marranos (secret Jews) and other compromised believers expiated their guilt by chanting the *Kol Nidre*.

Why then, is the *Kol Nidre* so important that is must be performed three times, so latecomers will not miss hearing a complete statement of it? Why is it so important that the entire evening service, in most congregations, has come to be known by its name as in, "Don't be late, remember next Tuesday evening is *Kol Nidre*."

The answer is not to be found in its text so much as it is to be discovered in its subtext. If this nullification has to do only with those vows made between human beings and God, one has to delve into what kinds of vows are made between an individual and God.

Consider the following menu: Marriage vows, vows to good health and away from compulsive disorders, vows to become a better informed, more spiritual person, vows not to commit those little murders of uncaring indecency and lack of friendship to one's self and others, vows not to steal another person's thunder or recognition, vows not be greedy and so on.

In other words, *Kol Nidre's* text of legal nullification between vows made between God and us, leads to the far deeper subtext of our confronting our own ultimate weaknesses and shortcomings before the Almighty. We are naked before God and each and every one of our most despised blemishes is on garish display.

We are ashamed and beg for compassionate leniency and forgiveness for what we hoped would be a proud accomplishment of a year but turned out to be, at times, a miserable failure and a wasted effort.

There is another subtext to *Kol Nidre*. Since we were children we were taken by our parents to this awe-filled service where we not only experienced our own faults but saw our parents, revealed, perhaps for the first time, as vulnerable, imperfect human beings as well.

We might look over at them during the *Kol Nidre* and realize how they are growing older and are frailer than last year. How will they fare in the coming year? Or, if they have passed away, our own aging and mortality might flood our thoughts.

Often the surrounding environment and conditions in which a text is presented may influence a deeper sub-textual resonance having nothing to do with the actual text but everything to do with its most primal impact upon us.

Every literary idea in our prayers has the possibilities of several sub-textual meanings beneath it.

They may be a sense of innocence underneath a supplication, grateful relief under a prayer of thanks, mystery under a memorial, or anxiety under a sense of awe.

When searching for the right subtext, we ask ourselves: What is it about this text that attracts me and concerns me at the same time? What is the dual nature of this text? What primal feelings of fear, joy, mystery, gratitude, anxiety, anger or sensuality are called up within us as we listen to the music and the words?

We consider its musical setting. Does it enhance or work against that primal sense in us. Whatever the sub-textual meaning we've chosen to focus upon, we wonder does this music clarify and intensify that sub-textual mood?

It may not address the literal subject, but it will add much greater depth to the text if these hidden meanings are revealed to us. This may sound complex, but it needn't be at all. Let me offer an example. I've set the *Sh'ma* - "the watchword of our faith" several times in various services. Every time that I set it I try to find another sub-text to comment upon or to use in clarifying the text.

In my sacred service *Hegyon Libi* (Meditation of My Heart), I set the *Sh'ma* very quietly almost coaxing each listener to strain a bit to listen or "Hear O Israel," until I effect a great crescendo on the work *echad*, oneness, unity. My sub-textual connection is that quietly listening to each other's differences will finally scream out to us that we are really not that different at all but all of the same kind; and kindness promotes oneness.

Play recorded example #9—*Sh'ma* from *Hegyon Libi* sung by Cantor Roslyn Barak

On another occasion, in a service entitled *L'maaseih V'reisheet* (To Recreate the World), attaching the previous prayer *Ahavat Olam* (Love for the World) I set the *Sh'ma* as a fanfare almost introducing *Adonai, Eloheinu* to the listener as if for the first time as a direct result of the love between us.

Play recorded example #10—*Ahavat Olam/Sh'ma* from *L'maaseih V'reisheet* (To Recreate the World) sung by Cantor Mark Childs.

This sub-textual musical *midrashic* setting suggests that no matter how many times we recognize God's name in the Bible or in the prayer book, until we get to know Godliness (loving the world and its inhabitants) in our own personal lives, as if for the very first time, we really don't hear God's presence in the deepest most meaningful sense at all.

With only three basic themes to the *Sh'ma*; First - Hear O Israel, second - *Adonai* is our God, and third - *Adonai* is One, each of these subjects can project several subtexts.

For example: "*Sh'ma Yisrael*, Hear O Israel" How and what does one truly hear: Is Israel the only people required to hear about *Adonai*? Is hearing, without doing, enough to achieve unity? ...And so on.

Finding subtexts is not difficult. The creative challenge for us will be to find the one that speaks most personally to us and to appreciate its musical attitude as an enhancement of this symbolism. One might very well wonder if these subtexts are more important than the surface text or story, why bother creating a surface text in the first place? Why not just cut to the sub-textual meaning and save everybody time and effort.

The answer is that it is precisely the time and effort spent by us in searching for and understanding our personal, particular sub-textual connection to an impersonal objective text or story that makes it valuable in our own specific life and most necessary as a prayer.

A good story or text is filled with multi-level meanings and subtexts. A good musical composition or accompaniment is also rich in sub-textual considerations. Understanding the richness of each texture and the relationship between the music and the words increases as we access multi-leveled *midrashic* interpretations

The seventh and final dramatic principle in sacred music is:

7. **Value music that uses dramatic opposition to access *midrashic* interpretation.**

Every subject, no matter how clear-cut it seems at first, has a greater *midrashic* meaning carrying with it many shadings that are frequently at dramatic opposition to each other.

Dramatic opposites are everywhere, surrounding us in everyday life. They are not just exemplified in intense and gripping musical settings. Most often they are reflections of the ironic human nature.

The *Jewish Week* Israel correspondent Joshua Mitnick reports a fascinating phenomenon:

> Tel Aviv — The bar borrows its name from an American war hero in Iraq. The décor is punctuated with photographs of Afghan Taliban men. The music fuses house rhythms with lilting Arabic melodies from the canon of Egyptian diva Umm Kulthum.

Proof that the concept works can be found on the dance floor at Shoshana Johnson's, where twenty-something Israelis swivel their hips and jubilantly raise their arms like Middle Eastern folk dancers. "The sexiest and most effervescent [bar] around," according to a local entertainment guide.

Normally fixated on emulating New York and European chic, the music and culture of Israel's adversaries have become the new trend on Tel Aviv's bar scene. Long ignored as parochial and melancholy, Arabic music is now embraced as party music by Tel Aviv's fashionable set…

"Lots of people here think we are European or we are on the standard with Americans. But the fact is that we are here in the Middle East and are sitting next to Arab neighbors." …

"If there were terrorist attacks left and right there's no way I could play this music," said Oren Alkalay, the co-owner of Mishmish, which hosts an Arabic music night every week. "It would be a very naïve thing to do, to be listening to the music of your enemy."…

"We live in a cruel reality. The bubble is very important of what we have here," he said. "We're in the business of making a good time — people go out and drink alcohol and feel good."

How is that for dramatic opposition? A tourist to Tel Aviv expecting to hear *chalutz* (pioneer) songs, *horas* (circle dances), Israeli patriotic or love ballads, or even the songs of Naomi Shemer (the matriarch of Israeli song) goes for a drink in a recommended popular Tel Aviv night spot and watches young Israelis joyfully dancing to the Arabic music of their enemies?

On a *pshat* level it makes no sense. On this level it seems that the state of Israel's pride has been terribly discounted by the young who no longer can be counted on to support the hopes and dreams of the Jewish homeland.

Because of this glaring, dramatic, irregularity, the interpretive work must begin, at the very least, on the level of *remez*; some aspect is hidden. Adding a *drash*, one of the interviewed commented that this young generation's new paradigm is not European, or American culture but the region's indigenous Arabic culture. However, on the level of *sod*, there is an even more profound meaning. Anyone who has ever lived in a minority community understands this secretive interpretation. It is that victims often identify as much with those who cause their suffering as much as they do with their fellow vanquished.

Young Israelis, from the time they go out in the streets, live with the reality that their best friends as well as members of their immediate and extended families, may be senselessly blown up by Palestinians who have been taught at an early age not to care for their own lives on earth.

What do we tell young swimmers who are afraid of drowning? Confront your worst fear and dive back into the water. What do we tell a rider who has fallen off a horse? Get right back on.

These young Israelis, know too well the fragility of life and the omnipresence of death waiting them in the army and on the streets.

In an effort to function and triumph over their deepest anxieties they confront them on the dance floor in the music of the *Intifada* (Palestinian uprising). They revel in its surrogate danger and emerge from the dance floor victorious and still alive bolstered by the temporary conquering of their fear. They have met the enemy head on! On this midrashic level of interpretation the irony of this Arab dance music in Tel Aviv seems almost logical. We empathize and want to join them in their choreographed battle.

From the simultaneity of time *midrash*, young Israeli Jews who have been emotionally scarred in the past, dance bravely in the present visualizing a time in the future when they and their Arab neighbors will truly dance together in friendship. This generation has hardly given up hope.

They have creatively approached it from another angle and yearn for peace as fervently as their elders do.

Consider a similar scenario in the Bible when the Children of Israel also danced to Egyptian music: Moses is descending from Mount Sinai with the two tablets of the Law. He hears and then sees the Children of Israel dancing around the Golden Calf and he throws the tablets at them in anger smashing the tablets to bits.

There are three beats or divisions to this scene: Moses' initial descent, his first awareness of the dancing, and his climactic destructive action.

How does a composer musically depict this scene in the most dramatic way while also adding a *drash* or commentary of his own to the scenario? How does music make this biblical history "come alive"?

Recognizing and analyzing the negative space, the composer considers each obvious contrasting emotion and uses these contrasting opposites as fodder for a dramatic setting.

For example: Moses is descending Mount Sinai. For forty days he has not been resting. His proximity with God throughout the forty days has probably caused his adrenalin to continually pump while he furiously takes dictation from the Lord. Upon his descent, he is undoubtedly exhausted and in deep meditation. Which type of music should a composer employ in setting this moment - tired music or its negative space thrilling, energetic music?

Though Moses is thoroughly exhausted, the skillful composer would play the dramatic opposite mood; that is, an energetic optimistic music, based on biblical cantillation, to comment upon how God's law has invigorated the Children of Israel's leader with hope for the structure for his people's communal future.

Even in his exhaustion there is the negative space of tremendous energy thrilled by the quality of the holy mission in which he has been immersed. Dramatically, the composer has also set up the scene of a hopeful Moses descending the mountain.

Then Moses sees the Golden Calf. Before his rage boils to the point of throwing down the tablets, what do you think his initial reaction would be? Does he immediately explode or is there a contrasting process underscored in the music?

Imagine that Moses hears the Egyptian songs and dances (after all, the worship of the Golden Calf is a regression back to slavery in Egypt) and this music is the opposite of the holiness in the cantillation that he feels descending Mount Sinai. Consequently, an insightful composer might play the disintegration of that Torah chant inspired music that we have initially heard. Through distortion of intervals and rhythms one might create a bizarre cantillation reflecting Moses' confusion at his people's actions and the grotesque quality of this vision.

Finally, if the depiction of the actual throwing of the tablets was dramatized for television, there would be the usual action packed underscore music as the tablets crumble, the people scurry, the calf is destroyed and Moses and the people anguish in their misery.

This, though, would be a *pshat*, literal interpretation encouraging a lower common denominator of music scoring.

Where is the negative space?

What is not being shown at this moment of mortal fury?

What is the musical *midrash* that could truly define and intensify the tragic sadness of this lack of faith?

In an interesting commentary, it might be God's reaction to it all by His quiet weeping at the disappointment of His divine plan being ruined by human weakness and lack of belief.

The skillful composer would use this opposite dramatic effect, to play against the violent action, perhaps in a slow, mournful string orchestra elegy, similar to the *Adagio for Strings* by Samuel Barber, as if God was looking down and crying. All the movement of the violent action on the ground would be seen (and heard) in a contrapuntal aerial perspective in opposition with God's sad lament.

These dramatically effective compositional strategies of opposition are derived from the awareness that each positive shape (or musical gesture) is also defined by negative space (or contrasting, opposing, musical attitude).

The result of the marriage between the positive and negative is a heightened super-reality as well as the inclusion of a third element (in this case God's sense of disappointment), which comments upon the initial relationship.

When we, as listeners, consider music depicting biblical events, which include a *midrash* incorporating negative space, we can now appreciate what it dramatically accomplishes. By suggesting alternatives, extensions, treatments, developments, and, above all, commentary about the subject matter at hand music gives it three-dimensional life.

This awareness enriches our appreciation of Jewish music created for this purpose and accesses its meditation upon the larger issue; God's presence in defining and adding insights of clarity in the space connecting us with our humanity.

I give credit and express my gratitude to the memory of my teacher Lehman Engle who stressed this device while I studied with him in the BMI Musical Theatre Workshop many years ago in New York. Maestro Engle would illustrate this concept of dramatic opposition with a scene from *Fiddler on the Roof*. There, Tevye, a poor dairyman who struggles everyday to support his wife and five daughters, prays to God for sustenance to exist on a meager, sub-standard of living.

He sings: *If I were a Rich Man*. Does he complain and grouse about how much his monthly costs are? No. Does he lament how his cow is old and can hardly give milk anymore? No. Does he even cry that his wife and daughters are in rags and he lives in a measly dwelling? No.

Why? Because nobody likes to root for a *kvetch*! (Yiddish for a whiner, a grumbler, a complainer, and a nudge!) There is nothing noble or heroic in complaining. You and I might do it in everyday life, but we are neither the protagonists of a Broadway musical nor, for that matter, the subjects of a prayer text setting.

So what does Tevye wish for and sing about if he was rich: First he'd sing a *nigun*, (a song without words - *bidi bidi bum*) in praise of God. Then he wouldn't have to work hard and he would discuss the holy books with the learned men by the Eastern Wall in the study house. He'd have a fancy house with staircases - one going up and the other going down. And, finally the payoff for being a rich man - people would ask his advice because "when you're rich they think you really know!"

All these are very funny allusions and endear Tevye to us as a man who can find humor in the midst of the cruelest conditions. Consequently, we like him very much and root for him to succeed.

When at the end, he and his family are uprooted from their *shtetl* (little village of Anatevka), we cry for them even more because they are noble even at the nadir of their misfortunes.

Fiddler on the Roof (even the irony of the title) is a classic use of opposites in developing a characterization dramatically and empathetically.

•

When I came to Los Angeles after earning a Ph.D. in composition from the Eastman School of Music, in order to compose for television and films, I began a "post doctoral apprenticeship" working as an orchestrator for some of Hollywood's best film composers including Alex North, Elmer Bernstein, and Walter Scharf. I also studied composing for television with the gifted and highly successful composer and arranger Earle Hagen.

Mr. Hagen advocated parallel composing for television. If the scene was sad he'd advise write sad music, and if the scene was happy he'd say write happy music. He advocated this parallel style of composition because television didn't want you to think so much as to become anesthetized and stay tuned through all the commercials as a passive commercial consumer.

However, in feature film music scores, dramatic opposites and scoring the subtext always came into play. It was understood that we were willing, captive viewers in the movie theatre and wouldn't run off to the kitchen for a snack or change channels with our remotes.

Filmmakers, therefore, allowed us the luxury of considering the movie as an art form complete with ironies, opposites, dualities and multi-levels of meaning.

Seemingly opposite dualities are nothing new to the Jewish experience. Diaspora Jews have lived for centuries in the dual capacities of Jew and citizen of their particular host country. Language, laws, customs, dress, lifestyles and cultural affinities have all demonstrated fascinating dualities and, sometimes, tragic ones.

To survive the Inquisition and other religious persecutions, *Marranos* outwardly converted during the Middle Ages in Portugal to Catholicism while secretly practicing Judaism behind the closed shutters of their homes. It may also be noted that more Jews would have survived Hitler's gas chambers if they did not believe so strongly and patriotically in nationalism, the primacy and integrity of their dual identities as both Jews and patriotic citizens of the state.

They remained in their homes because they were not only Jews but also citizens of their fatherland who fought bravely for it in former wars.

Jews live with contradictions and those opposites that often make up the other side of the same coin; it is part of our heritage.

Often a musical affect in opposition to the literary one suggests a different time or place. For example, I've composed several songs for baby namings; one was for a boy called *B'ni* (My Son) composed for my older son Ari's naming and, another, *Biti* (My Daughter) to insure equanimity and parity when my wife Suzy was pregnant with our second child. Little did I know, that my second child Andy would also be a boy. Today, Andy, a strapping six-foot tall man with a keen sense of humor, good-naturedly refers to *Biti* as his song.

The point concerning the creation of these songs is that when I composed the setting of *B'ni*, I took the opposing dualities of Torah cantillation as chanted by a mature male and framed it with an *Alberti Bass* (a simple arpeggiation) in the treble range suggesting a cradle song for a newborn infant.

As I named my son Ari Lev after my father, Aryeh Leib[z"l], I held our infant in my arms, remembered my own beginnings, and optimistically projected ahead to a time when this beautiful baby would grow strong and do us proud as a knowledgably aware, capable *Ba'al Korei* (The designated public Torah chanter) as both he and his brother did accomplish so well later on in their lives.

•

The text for **B'ni is** from Proverbs III, 1- 6.

B'ni, torati al tishkach umitzvotai yitsor libecha.

My son, do not forget my Torah;

But let your heart keep my commandments.

Ki orech yamim ush'not chayim v'shalom yosifu lach.

They shall add length of days, long life, and peace to you.

Chesed veemet al yaazvucha;

Let mercy and truth not forsake you;

kashreim al garg'rotecha, katveim al luach libecha;

Bind them about your neck, write them upon the table of your heart;

um'tsa chein v'seichel tov b'einei Elohim v'adam.

So shall you find favor and good understanding in the eyes of God and man.

B'tach el Adonai b'chol libecha v'el binatcha al tishaein.

Trust in the Lord with all your heart rather than lean on your own understanding.

B'chol d'rachecha daeihu v'hu y'yasher orchotecha.

In all your ways acknowledge God who will smooth your path.

Play recorded example #11- B'ni sung by Cantor Faith Steinsnyder

In contrast, when I composed *Biti* (My Daughter), my image for this infant girl was very different. It was that of holding a little baby daughter and envisioning a time when she would grow to be an elegantly beautiful bride whom I would escort down the aisle to her handsome groom at the canopy. Again the simplicity of a cradlesong interacted in an opposing attitude with downward melodic sweeps, which are both sensual and sophisticated suggesting a beautiful woman descending a staircase as a bride.

Before feminists write to me in protest, let me objectively, emphatically and fully acknowledge the total equality of talent, innate ability, and scholarship of women in Jewish intellectual life. Whether as rabbis, cantors, or laypersons this equality (or superiority) gives them the absolute ability and right to choose a career over marriage and children or the dual burden of both.

My pre-compositional reverie of a Jewish Cinderella was in no way an objective reality but a composer's use of a romantic image as a device to help create a vivid *midrashic* image for a baby girl. I then used that dramatic conceit to compose a lyrical song where none existed before. I'm certain that the thousands of people who have heard *Biti* sung since then have made different, varied, and contrasting associations tangential to their own experiences.

Parenthetically, when I researched scripture to find a suitable text for *Biti*, aside from the slave labor images of *Eishet Chayil – A Woman of Valor*, I could not find a single text about the nobility of daughters in our literature. There is a dearth of source material in our traditional texts relating to women. This is why so much mythic material has arisen surrounding the Madonna in Christian scripture.

I was fortunate to befriend Rabbi Kerry Baker who subsequently authored an original text in the style of scripture. *Biti*, published and recorded in celebration of Megan Turkat's Bat Mitzvah, at University Synagogue, Los Angeles, California, went on to express many parents' parental love and blessings for their daughters. Here's the lovely text by Rabbi Kerry Baker:

Biti, ki at han'shama beineinu,

My daughter, because you are the soul between us,

Biti, ki at shalom v'shalvah,

My daughter, because you are peace and tranquility,

Biti, ki at haruach b'veiteinu,

My daughter, because you are the spirit of our home

Iti at tishari ad olam.

You will remain within our hearts forever.

Boi yaldah nilmad torat ameinu,

Come, my child let us learn the Torah of our people.

Boi yaldah nifgosh et haolam,

Come, my child let us meet the world.

Boi yaldah b'meshech kol chayeinu,

Come, my child, throughout our lives

Neileich al darchei noam.

Let us walk in paths of pleasantness.

Ahavti yaldati otach,

We have loved you, our daughter

Mipnei shebat kivracha elai;

For you have brought us blessing.

Asim al rosheich et birkat yadi.

We place upon your head the blessings of our hands.

Biti, ki at ohevet et horayich,

My daughter, knowing your love for your parents,

Yaldati, ki at neehav baElohim,

My child, knowing you are loved by God,

Eitein yaldah ahavati eilayich,

We give, daughter, our love to you,

V'eitein lach birkat libi - biti.

And with it, Daughter, the blessing of our hearts.

Play recorded example #12- *Biti* sung by Cantor Faith Steinsnyder

I recently had occasion to re-screen the wonderful movie *Forrest Gump*. It tells the story of one of the more complicated periods in America's recent history.

The nation was fighting an unpopular war in Viet Nam, the Presidency's integrity was crumbling, drugs were rampant and AIDS was coming into our consciousness; the society was literally unraveling before our eyes. How does one best tell this story of a truly tumultuous period?

The genius of Robert Zemekis, its filmmaker, is that he completely and most creatively understood dramatic opposites. He tells the story through the perceptions of Forrest Gump, a simple boy who grows up to be a simple man.

Forrest is one who understands the polarities of life in the clearest, most absolute ways; there are few gray areas in his mind. He follows orders, knows right from wrong, good from bad, and as he says: "I might not be the smartest person, but I do know love."

How refreshing a point of view this cinematic work possesses. Certainly Gump is larger than life. We root for him constantly and applaud when he resolutely responds to: "Are you stupid?" with "Stupid is as stupid does!"

As a loving son, a football hero, saving Lieutenant Dan's life, winning the Medal of Honor, becoming an international ping-pong champion, meeting three U.S. presidents, becoming fabulously wealthy, he seems to be just the opposite; a very wise man in simple man's garb living a fulfilled life.

From the moment he begins his incredible narrative while waiting for the Savannah bus, through its repetitive, periodic returns, to Jenny's episodic appearances, the progress of the story is clear as a bell.

When he finally marries Jenny and experiences joy with her and their son, conflicted reality strikes and she dies too soon. Forrest's simple monologue at her grave under the beautiful tree is as touching a moment in film as one could hope for.

The movie ends with the bookends of the older Forrest waiting with his son the younger Forrest for the school bus as his Mama did with him at the film's opening and the feather blowing in the wind as the unifying cadence. The drama of *Forrest Gump* sums up a well-made story and both an intellectually and emotionally satisfying dramatic experience. It engages us, makes us wonder, weep, and feel gratitude for being alive.

It has all the seven dramatic principles beautifully typified and is a great object lesson. These seven are the fundamentals of good story telling because they help us appreciate the deeper *midrash* of compositional narratives.

In this chapter we have studied how the seven principles of drama influence the best sacred music settings culminating with the final principle of dramatic opposition.

If a text is sad, a skillful composer, instead of opting for a parallel setting with sad music, creates music that is bittersweet, or even hopeful. If a text deals with a complicated idea, it might be set simply. If a text is simple, it might be given a musical underpinning or patina of importance to bolster it. If a text is joyous, it might be tempered by an additional quality of excitement, mystery, or poignancy to round it out.

The best sacred music settings do not parallel the main emotional characteristic of the text with the main emotional characteristic of the music. These settings are in "complimentary contrast" with each other.

In summary, one of religion's jobs is to explain nature and human nature by means of effective storytelling. Whether at religious services, in books, at the theatre or ballet, on television, in the movies, or in the personal transactions of our day-to-day lives, we love stories.

We make decisions about relationships and the need for new "chapters" in our lives based on the desire to tell others new stories about ourselves and not to repeat or hear the same old stories from others. Our most intimate, personal relationships with God are often illustrated in great mythic proportions.

All the dramatic principles that we have discussed are founded on the idea that a dramatic story or a musical story called a composition should be told clearly and vividly, meaning it should be larger than life, have an engaging beginning, clear road maps along the way, and an appropriately clear ending.

By creating a larger than life conception, finding a point of view that is fresh, letting us know the nature of the work we are about to experience, and reminding us what we have just experienced with intelligent repetition, a composer delineates and emphasizes what is important. Reminders also give us familiar material and the momentary freedom to re-process and re-interpret the new musical data that we are receiving in a *midrashic* way.

Chapter 11
The *Midrash* of Liturgical Music

Prayer is meaningless unless it is subversive, unless it seeks to overthrow and to ruin the pyramids of callousness, hatred, opportunism and falsehood. The liturgical movement must become a revolutionary movement, seeking to overthrow the forces that continue to destroy the promise, the hope, and the vision. — *Abraham Joshua Heschel, On Prayer*

Before addressing the "revolutionary" aspect of prayer (and liturgical music) that Abraham Joshua Heschel writes about, an understanding of traditional roots is necessary. One cannot write about traditional Jewish liturgical (worship) music without mentioning its guiding forces: cantillation, the tropes or melodic formulas used in chanting the *Tanach;* and *nusach hat'filah,* melodic motives used in the traditional improvised chanting of Jewish prayers. But, first a word about the idea of tradition itself.

Tradition is a highly subjective and temporal idea. Composer Samuel Adler notes, "Tradition is what you know from last year." When you think about it; it is true. What we have already learned, have come to experience and know, and, above all, feel comfortable with, we call *traditional.* By the same token, blind customs, beliefs, and actions that cannot be identified or explained, including music that we cannot attribute with any authority to a particular composer, we also call *traditional.*

Furthermore, with greater knowledge of national and ethnic sub-divisions within Judaism, what is known as traditional for a Sephardic Jew from Morocco may well be totally foreign to an Ashkenazic Jew from Poland. In a heterogeneous congregation, which tradition takes precedence as more traditional? Sephardic? Ashkenazic? Oriental? Yemenite? Summer Camp? Ethiopian? Whose tradition? From what country, and which town? When in their history? Interpreted by whom? And on and on. Let me share with you one of my favorite stories about tradition:

> During a service at an old synagogue in Eastern Europe, when the Sh'ma prayer was said, half the congregants stood up and half remained seated.
>
> The half that was seated started yelling at those standing to sit down, and the ones standing yelled at the ones sitting to stand up.
>
> The rabbi, learned as he was in the Law and commentaries, didn't know what to do. His congregation suggested that he consult a housebound ninety-eight year old man who was one of the original founders of their temple. The rabbi hoped the elderly man would be able to tell him what the actual temple tradition was, so he went to the nursing home with a representative of each faction of the congregation.
>
> The one whose followers stood during Sh'ma said to the old man, "Is the tradition to stand during this prayer?" The old man answered, "No, that is not the tradition."
>
> The one whose followers sat said, "Then the tradition is to sit during Sh'ma!"
>
> The old man answered, "No, that is not the tradition." Then the rabbi said to the old man, "But the congregants fight all the time, yelling at each other about whether they should sit or stand."
>
> The old man interrupted, exclaiming, "That's the tradition!"

•

Traditions used to be hundreds of years old. However, with "future shock" and information overload, modern traditions are much newer, briefer, and less enduring. With the rapidity of contemporary life, tradition might be what we know from last year, but will it still be traditional next year?

Furthermore, what is the correct aesthetic balance for Jewish music programming in the present? Should our music reflect the past predominantly, as a *sofer's* (a Torah scribe) creativity does? Should the musical program be set in stone, as it is in the Lewandowsky music exclusively employed by the Berlin Rykestrasse Synagogue? Should it only reflect the immediate, "trendy" present, as the camping movement in Reform Judaism does? Should our devotional music push us more into the exhilarating turmoil of exploring the future? Or should it — can it not help — be an eclectic mix that combines all three?

Should Jewish music be individually steadfast in elevating us by its *midrashic* potential? Should it, alternatively, primarily serve congregants who, in the name of tradition, are often quite happy passively hearing the same finite, though lesser, repertoire of known, comfortable compositions again and again *ad infinitum*?

When most of us ask for something fresh and new in our worship services, we are usually asking not for a *shir chadash* (a new song) but new music that sounds like an old familiar one, most reflective of our personal tradition from our own childhood and neighborhood, in the performance style of the *Hazzan* of our youth. Just as constant change is unnerving, traditions in stone are, of course, a death knell for the organic growth and advancement of our hearts and minds and ... Jewish music.

This is why, in focusing attention on two of these traditional Jewish music systems, there is an ambivalence and even some conflict about how much importance to attribute to "traditional" musical materials that include *cantillation* and *nusach hat'filah*.

On the one hand, knowing these sounds and appreciating their place in our music gives our worship a unique sense of historicity and authenticity. On the other hand, it is not enough merely to quote and requote them. Unless today's cantors and composers are trained in the skill of transforming and customizing cantillation and *nusach* motives within their own personal compositional or improvisational idioms, music based on these traditional materials can sound clichéd, repetitive, and, at worst, trite.

Once again, I include a caveat before introducing these two systems. Each of these areas is a multi-leveled, complex study, which needs at least a full book of its own to comprehend fully. As before, I will venture to introduce them to you with Hillel's recommendation, *"Tsei ul'mad"* (Go and continue studying each of them in greater detail to fully appreciate their profound liturgical influence).

First, let us address the oldest of these two sound systems, biblical cantillation. This means, literally, the reader's or *baal koreh's* chant, based on the realization of the trope symbols, or *ta'amei mikrah,* used in the public chanting of the Torah, Prophets, and additional scrolls.

For an in depth investigation, the reader will enjoy Joshua R. Jacobson's highly detailed *Chanting the Hebrew Bible: The Art of Cantillation,* published in the abridged version by The Jewish Publication Society.

Pragmatically, the more user friendly immediate information on this subject comes in smaller books including Samuel Rosenbaum's *A Guide to Torah Reading,* published by KTAV Publishing and *Biblical Chant,* by Abraham Wolf Binder (Hebrew Union College, Sacred Music Press, New York, 1959) for all the college's cantorial students learning to chant. It is available on line from Transcontinental Music Publications, New York. Binder, who learned and simplified his system by studying Solomon Rosowsky's system, *The Cantillation of the Bible,* (The Reconstructionist Press, New York, 1957), takes you step by step through the entire

Ashkenazic system. If you are interested in learning and mastering the system, these books will teach you all that you need to know. The following brief history of cantillation is adapted from Binder's introduction.

Historically, our ancestors knew early on that through melody, words were remembered and understood more clearly. In 444 BCE, after the second Temple was destroyed and Israel returned from captivity in Babylon, the Torah and its accompanying scripture was chanted in the marketplace during weekdays (Mondays and Thursdays). Later, it was chanted in synagogues on Shabbat and during the three festivals.

Chanters first used a system of hand signals called "chironomy." The chanter's assistant would stand beside the chanter's desk and use hand signals to indicate the rise and fall of the melody. This helped the chanter recall and affect the three basic divisions of each sentence, the beginning, middle, and end.

Later more symbols were added to refine and specify more subtle textual meanings. For illustrations of chironomy read *The Roots of Biblical Chant* by Richard Neumann (Board of Jewish Education of Greater New York, 1982).

It was in the setting up and elaboration of these beginning, middle, and final structural tropes that subtleties of *midrash* became possible. Words that could be interpreted in more than one way were properly emphasized and contextualized by the trope assigned to it. If one trope was more dramatic and colorful than another, that word which was assigned to it, gained immeasurably in importance.

The Talmud tells us that, in the first century of the common era, about five hundred years after the beginning of public chanting, the Torah should not only be sung in public but with a special system of chant, but that it should sound quite different and apart from secular melodies.

With continuous cross-pollination of liturgical and musical ideas between Judaism and other religions the system of trope developed, as discussed and documented in Eric Werner's *The Sacred Bridge* (Columbia University Press, 1959) and Maestro Joel Cohen's recording *The Sacred Bridge: Jews and Christians in Medieval Europe* (Erato (France) CD 2292-45513-2). Between the fifth and ninth centuries the Ben Asher family in Tiberias, Palestine, codified the system of punctuation and cantillation that has come down to us today.

Every scriptural book now read in public has a distinct melodic profile based on this system of tropal symbols. They include the Torah, Prophets, Scrolls of Esther, Lamentations, Ruth, Ecclesiastes, Song of Songs, Psalms, and in some communities, Job. Only Proverbs, Ezra, Nehemiah and Chronicles have no special melodic formulas, because they are not chanted in public. Think of it! Every syllable of the thousands of words in the Torah and most of its accompanying books are set to music, and each book has a different melody.

The system itself is remarkable and elegantly simple. There are twenty-eight tropes, or signs. Nineteen, called Lords or Disjunctives, set and clarify the key words and syllables in each sentence. Nine are called Servants or Conjunctives. These prepare or musically set up the Disjunctive. Each book is distinguished by a specific modality (melody) .

Recorded example #13 demonstrates Torah cantillation for chanting the Five Books of Moses. This trope is the Mannheim variety that I learned and taught to my own sons know familiarly as the *Mapach-Pashta*. This one group contains all the tropal motives.

Play example #13—Mannheim Torah cantillation chanted by Michael Isaacson

Recorded example #14 demonstrates the *Haftarah* cantillation for chanting the Prophets, in the Ashkenazic tradition, employing the same visual tropes but using the Prophetic melodic system.

Play recorded example #14—Ashkenazic Haftarah cantillation chanted by Michael Isaacson

As we listen, we understand how the different sounds of each book can facilitate the memorization of the respective texts. But, knowing this system of tropes does not necessarily mean singing the same melodies as other Jewish communities using the same tropal system. In 1968, when I first went to Israel and studied Jewish music at Hebrew University in Jerusalem, I met Professor Avigdor Herzog. At that time he was collecting and transcribing recorded samples by all the Torah chanters from each Jewish community that he could find of the first paragraph of Genesis. Knowing that vocal ornamentations and variations develop during the course of an oral art, his purpose was to discover, through the variations and the similarities of this personalization, the migration patterns of these communities. Chants were an oral tradition, passed from one generation to another. It made sense that one community's chant, which was similar to another's, had more of a kindred relationship than two whose chants were markedly contrasted.

How fascinating that a relatively simple system had, through time, generated literally hundreds of variations. I remember chanting for Professor Herzog the torah trope that I had learned from my teacher, Rabbi Hillel Hochberg in Brooklyn, New York, which later I taught to my two sons in Los Angeles, California. He quickly identified it as trope from Mannheim, Germany. Astonishing! This meant that my teacher's teacher or his teacher came from Mannheim and transposed the original geographical identity of the trope to an entirely different location, as I had continued to do. Because of the breadth of geographic migration today, how could Herzog's system be an accurate contemporary indicator?

Sh'mot Hataamim "Zarka Table" - Haftarah
Names and Order of the Tropal Motives for Chanting the Prophets

Notated by Michael Isaacson
Based on Samuel Rosenbaum's interpretation

Note: There are no *shalshelet, yerach ben yomo,* or *karnei farah* signs in the Haftarah. The *mercha ch'fula* has the same melody as in the Torah trope.

© 2007 Michael Isaacson, ECM Music (ASCAP)

We can now understand how this academic study can become fascinatingly complex. Where does authenticity begin or end and which is the most authentic tradition, yours, mine, or both?

You will enjoy listening to Leonard Bernstein's use of both the Haftarah trope and Lamentations trope in his *Jeremiah Symphony,* the scherzo and the third movement respectively, (He composed it when he was only twenty-two.) Listen as in each movement he begins literally and then transmutes the tropal motifs to meld with his more personal, contemporary compositional idiom.

179

Finally, one does not have to compose only liturgical or classical music to borrow successfully from the tropes. The talented lyricist Susan Nurenberg[z″l] and I were once asked to write a children's Purim song about Esther the Queen. I decided it would be fun and educational to put the musical sound of Purim, the cantillation for reading the *Megillah* (the scroll of Esther) into an accessible song so that the children learned both the words and the Purim cantillation. In recorded example #15 *Esther the Queen* accomplishes this task.

Play recorded example #15 *Esther the Queen* sung by Cantor Faith Steinsnyder

In summing up cantillation's role as part of musical *midrash* in our worship services, there is no doubt that those who first set the tropes to the text were adding their layer of interpretation to the written word. It is also clear that the tempo, accentuation, and melodic inflections now used by accomplished *baalei koreh*, experienced Torah chanters, adds drama, emphasis, and *gravitas* to individual words and phrases. The Ashkenazic system is codified to the extent that its use is recognizable in cantorial improvisations, and composed music. There are still great interpretive variations possible. Compositionally, this musical system has hardly been explored as an abstraction. There is great room for its expansion and development in this compositional arena in the future.

•

We continue now with a brief history and some introduction to the second traditional Jewish musical system *nusach hat'filah*, a cantorial system of improvisation.

Though the role of the cantor logically evolves after the Babylonian dispersion in 586 BCE, when synagogue services replace temple sacrifices, *Hazzanut* (the art of the cantor) as we now recognize it may be traced back to Germany in 1220 and Süsskind von Trimberg. Trimberg was a minnesinger, a traveling musician akin to a Johnny Appleseed of music. He learned a song in one town and introduced it in another. In reality, he was probably a *badchin*, a wedding singer who entertained the bride and groom and their guests. Since all *badchins* had good voices, retentive memories, and were highly trained in the available repertoire, it is a good guess that Süsskind ("a sweet child") was either quite familiar with liturgical music or moonlighted as a *hazzan* himself.

In these Ashkenazic European communities, beginning in the Middle Ages melodic fragments became associated with specific services during the liturgical year. Adapting psalmody and other church musical motifs, *Hazzanim* serving as *Sh'lichei Tsibur* (messengers of the congregation before God) would chant unaccompanied prayer texts using these melodic fragments or motives made into scales and modes (displaced scales).

Eventually a *bel canto*, operatic style evolved, incorporating melismatic (many notes sung on one syllable) ornamentation derived from modal scales, which were constructed from and reflected these melodic fragments.

Listening to these oral compositions, a congregant could identify emotionally with the time of year, evening or morning, and the deeper sense of the prayer text upon the chronology of life.

Los Angeles pianist and composer Aminadav Aloni[z″l] used to explain *nusach* to his choir by passing along this *midrashic* tale:

There was a poor Jew who was wrongfully imprisoned in his village, and placed in solitary confinement in a cell with only a very small window near the ceiling. He was not allowed books or writing materials, but was able to keep track of time because he could hear the prayers emanating from the village synagogue nearby. By listening carefully and knowing the nusach for each of the services, he could tell whether it was a weekday or Shabbat, morning or evening, and when the seasonal holidays arrived, he knew which observances were being held by the fellow Jews in his village. This enabled him to maintain his humanity during his period of inhumane confinement.

To maintain the metaphor, we, Diaspora Jewry, might assess the value of *nusach* as aurally keeping us in touch with our Judaism in the imprisonment of our adopted secondary secular environment. These Jewish sounds bring us back to our parents' and grandparents' roots and provide continuity.

During the Baroque, Classical, and especially the Romantic time frames, the best *Hazzanim*, now called cantors (originally a non-Jewish church appellation), became known for their improvisatory virtuosity in *nusach hat'filah*. Their best improvisations were first passed down orally through appearances at synagogue concerts from town to town. At some point they were musically notated and recorded for others to study, emulate, and incorporate into their own quasi-improvisatory performing vocabulary. The Hazzan's craft, as we know the "traditional" Ashkenazic cantorial style, was codified during the past 250 years.

Today, most contemporary cantors learn their *nusach* and improvisatory *dreidels* (ornamental figures) in schools of sacred music, apprenticeship to more knowledgeable practitioners, by listening to recordings, or playing published cantorial collections by 19th and 20th century star cantor-educators. These include Sulzer, Baer, Katchko and, more recently, Koussevitsky, Alter, Ganchoff, Vinaver, Wohlberg, Spiro and Barkan. There are also several good texts available, lincluding Cantor Andrew Bernard' *The Sound of Sacred Time: A Basic Music Theory Textbook to Teach the Jewish Prayer*

Modes, used at Hebrew Union College in New York to codify the Ashkenazic practice.

Aside from weekday and special holiday *nuschaot,* there are three basic melodic modes used in *nusach,* named for prayers found in the *Kabbalat Shabbat,* the welcoming of the Sabbath service and the morning service. The texts which were first set to these modes are:

Adonai Malach (The Lord Reigns) - The modal scale is spelled with musical tones C, D, E, F, G, A, Bb, C, D#. It is basically a mixolydian mode with a raised ninth allowing both a major and minor third in the improvisation.

Magen Avot -(Shield of our Fathers). It is spelled C, D, Eb, F, G, Ab, Bb, C. It is a basic, natural minor scale.

Ahavah Rabah - (Great Love). Its mode is spelled C, Db, E natural, F, G, Ab, Bb, C. This mode is most popularly identified as "Jewish" in the non-Jewish world because of the exotic augmented second interval between the second and third steps and the harmonic flexibility between the Neapolitan relationship between the lowered second step and the tonic as contrasted by the whole step relationship between the lowered leading tone and the tonic.

•

The well-known Jewish songs *Hava Nagila, Eili, Eili,* and even Cole Porter's musical theatre song, *My Heart Belongs to Daddy* (Da, da, da, Da, da, da, Da, da da), are based on this *Ahavah Rabah* mode. Porter, not Jewish, was convinced that the best way to be successful as a New York songwriter was to sound "Jewish."

A cantor knew when each mode and which words in a prayer to emphasize. From this base, the cantor could begin in one mode and modulate, in any other part of the body of the text, either to another mode or to its major or minor parallel. The best cantorial improvisations are truly as inventive as jazz. As word painting was the basis for developing improvisations, by the words that were chosen as the improvisation's central focus, two cantors could chant the same prayer with the same *nusach* and evoke dramatically contrasting emotional responses and, each offer a distinctive musical midrash.

To add further spice to this system, and to comment on a specific text, cantors would often interpolate into the body of their improvisation *Misinai* or *Scarbova* tunes, meaning unattributed, anonymous folk melodies. These, presumably, were well known to their congregations and thought to be so immutable that they descended with Moses from Mount Sinai (the alternate term Scarbova appears to be derived from the Latin word for sacred). This Hazzan's respite from the solo gymnastics enabled the congregation to sing or hum along for the moment. For example, if Israel is being emphasized in the text, a melodic reference to *Hatikvah* might be used. While this is not the highest level of intellectual or artistic invention in improvisation, it is a useful device in keeping the congregation's attention and devotion refreshed, alert, and focused on the Hazzan's larger improvisatory spinning out of the prayer text.

A more sophisticated technique that combines *nusach* and *misinai* tunes is found in the German *Jahres Kaddish*. In this version of the *kaddish*, chanted by the Hazzan at the close of Yom Kippur during the *N'ilah* service (the closing of the metaphoric gates of heaven), before the gates are closed, the cantor culls melodic motifs from several versions of the *kaddish* sung throughout the year as a musical *midrashic* recapitulation of the year's occurrences.

For a more detailed description of the prayer modes and their use, the authoritative source of Jewish music, *Jewish Music in its*

Historic Development by Avraham Zvi Idelsohn and its companion text, *Jewish Liturgy* by A.Z. Idelsohn, (Schocken Books, New York), are highly recommended. Recordings by *Hazzanim* expert in *nusach* may be purchased on line.

When most people think of Jewish music, the first sounds that come to mind are the prayer settings, hymns, and holiday songs heard in the synagogue. This is as it should be. We grow up hearing these settings on a regular basis and become closely attached to them. The comfort of hearing them performed in the same manner each time is the essence of tradition; it provides stability in our lives and reinforces our identity of who we are.

As we grow and change in other areas of our lives and hopefully mature, most of us reassess our childhood music and replace some of it with grown-up music while others resist or prefer not to change. Through their static music they remain youngsters or summer campers, living in the past. In much liturgical music today, the comfort of the familiar often prevails over *midrashic* synagogue music settings that are more crafted. Even when better music is presented, many of us prefer the "oldies" simply because we grew up with them, and do not have to actively listen to it with adult ears and minds. We choose to stay children, musically.

However, to be fair, there is a more subtle process going on as well. Because the intellectual cognition of a well-known melody is immediately understood, it allows the congregant to make a brain shift from the "left side" (cognition) to the "right side" (emotive state), so that the listener can take flight and go off in a personal reverie.

It is one of the few times in worship when the rabbinic demand for "thinking" rather than "feeling" defines the worship experience. In modern times, however, thinking has often been overbalanced and taken back seat to mindless feelings of paroxysmal ecstasy.

Composing and choosing music for worship should not be undertaken in a casual manner. Settings created and sung simply because they possess a catchy tune or rhythm, are insufficient in satisfying the fundamental purpose for setting a prayer.

While the resulting music may still be infused with *ruach* (spirit), the underlying reason must surpass *keva* (structure and style). To reach spiritual heights, liturgical settings need to musically infuse the praises, pleas, and petitions of worship with a sense of *kavannah*, an informed intention of holiness and meaning in both the words and the music. The difference between the two is the difference between style and substance.

During the first half of the twentieth century, a Golden Age for the *Hazzan*, the congregation was encouraged to listen to both the rabbi and even more to the cantor, as much as participate. The great *Hazzanim* taught us *midrashic* musical lessons on a weekly basis. We were less in a hurry for instant gratification. One or two cantorial solos (*Hazzanut*) were always object lessons in *midrashic* text settings as we patiently and actively listened to the cantor's artful improvisation. Unfortunately, cantorial excesses and a lack of *Hazzanic* in-service growth forced the pendulum to swing in the opposite direction. Active listening was replaced with passive participation.

Now, those of us who seek a return to *midrashic* music, must parent ourselves. Before a musical work can even arrive at that substantive *midrashic* stage, basic imperatives of craft have to be met. The words have to be set correctly and with metric precision so that pronunciation is clear. Too frequently, liturgical musical settings for worship have incorrect accents on the wrong Hebrew syllables set to inappropriate music. Would we listen to or have respect for a rabbi who could not pronounce Hebrew or English correctly and chose to use distasteful street jargon during a sermon?

These are inadequacies that would impede the *kavannah* and the best communication of the rabbinic message. Why, then, do we make these concessions for liturgical music that is mis-accented and sung to inappropriate music? Why do we turn off our critical faculties when the cantor or congregation sings?

•

Perhaps it is because so much of our devotional aesthetic today has its roots in Hassidic music that is mis-accented and derived from street music. This religious movement was created by Israel ben Eliezer, who lived from 1698-1760, and was known as the *Baal Shem Tov* (Master of the Good Name).

Hassidism was an anti-intellectual reaction to the excessive *keva* of the *Mitnagdim* (literally the "opponents" of Hassidism), who advocated rational learning and literacy as a prerequisite for *kavannah*. Hassidism had a different philosophy. Literacy was not important nor a precondition; a worshipper merely needed emotional desire for a connection with God. Therefore, it was irrelevant if music did not function as *midrash* or even be stylistically appropriate.

Hassidism still employs music like the *nigun* (a highly repetitive wordless melody) to attain a state of religious euphoria. It is of no importance, in a Hassidic way of thinking, that music has its own language and syntax and *midrashic* potential. Hassidic music maintains the undistinguished task of being a nameless servant to the word. As long as any melody transports a Hassid to his desired worship state, casual street marches and secular dance music are interchangeably used for prayer settings without a second thought.

But we can do better. The rationales that "total participation throughout the service is the way to prayer" (Do we participate in the rabbi's sermon?) or "this is the music that is "in" (what is "in" today will surely be "out" tomorrow) or "the orthodox do it, so we can as well" (this is fine, if we are orthodox in every other aspect of our religious practice) are lesser considered, weaker rationales that rule out higher musical sensitivity, creativity and the realization of musical *midrash*. Worship music need not be devoid of intellect or critical assessment. We need not turn off our brains to turn on our hearts. Like every other example of elevated music that we cherish, worship music needs to be crafted with skill, knowingness, and sensitivity for language.

Teaching a class at Hebrew Union College, I pointed out to the student cantors that in the most popular, most often sung, traditional musical setting of *V'neemar* ("And it is said...."), in the concluding service, there are thirteen mis-accents in twelve measures of music.

Illustration #2 - lists the various ways that music is accented and then shows the musical notation for the popular sung version and one possible solution for correcting the mis-accents.

Though it is sung as the culmination of a Jewish worship service of prayer as a summation of all that we believe, we use a melody that is on the same plane with "The Farmer in the Dell." I doubt that the corrected adaptation that is offered in the illustration will ever replace the flawed version. M*inhag haBayit* (the custom of the house), even when patently incorrect, is extremely strong and obstinately enduring. While Samuel Adler has taught, "Tradition is what we know from last year," all cantors and music professionals in synagogue life will add that tradition is the most difficult bad habit to break.

I am not a fan of this traditional setting from a craftsman's point of view, or from one seeking some sense of intelligent *kavannah* in a text that is a culminating, dramatic expression of perfect belief.

Consider its words and the message:

V'ne-emar v'hayah Adonai l'Melech al kol haaretz

And it is said (written): God will be Sovereign over all the land.

Bayom hahu yih'yeh Adonai echad u'sh'mo Echad.

On that day, there will be one God whose name will be *Echad* (One).

This statement of hope and unity comes at the conclusion of our bending our knees in supplication before the Holy One. It is a fervent prayer that the dissension of the world will be replaced by a sure knowledge of who God is in our lives and our unified relationship with all humanity. It is a utopian wish for our highest ascent towards a cohesive nexus with our Creator.

Does this text warrant a nursery rhyme musical treatment? Is it a careless, militaristic, drinking song, or a lyrical anticipation of Judaism's highest fulfillment? Shouldn't we sing this with more *kavannah*, or as Samuel Adler has suggested, with an "adorned colloquialism?"

Melody is only one facet of music's profile. Rhythm, implied harmony, correct prosody, and modal color should also be considered when choosing an *a cappella* liturgical setting. The first step is to identify and minimize our use of poor settings. Let us examine the twelve-measure setting of *Bayom Hahu*, its thirteen mis-accentuations in the traditional setting, and an alternative remedy.

Recognizing and Correcting Misaccented Text Settings

Different types of accents
Dynamic Accent—Accentuation by singing the syllable louder or softer
Melodoc accent—Accentuation by setting the syllable on a dramatically higher or lower note
Agogic accent—Accentuation by holding the syllable for a longer duration

Timbral accent—Accentuation by changing the vocal timbre e.g. sotto voce, or falsetto

Textural accent—Accentuation by thickening or thinning the accompaniment

Traditional performance of V'ne-emar at the conclusion of the Alainu

There are thirteen mis-accentuations in twelve measures

M. 1—first accent of the word should be on "mar" not "ne"
M. 2—first accent of the word should be on "yah" not "ha"
M. 2—first accent of the word should be on "nai" not "A"
M. 3—secondary accent should be on "kol" not "al"
M. 5—"ha" should not receive a strong accent
M. 6—"ha" should not receive a strong accent
M. 6—"yi-h-yeh" has three syllables, not two
M. 7—first stress should be on "nai" not "A"
M. 7—"e" should not receive a long stress
M. 8—"u" should not receive a long stress
M. 9—"u" should not receive a long stress
M.10—"u" should not receive a long stress
M.11—"e" should not receive a long stress

A Possible Solution . . .

Play example #16—Traditionally sung *V'ne-emar*

Play example #17—Metrically correct *V'ne-emar*

As an alternative, recorded example #18 offers a metrically correct, *midrashic* setting in keeping with the text's lyrical hope that, when God's Kingdom is universal, we will ultimately understand the meaning and majesty of *Adonai's* holy name "One." Listen to *Bayom Hahu* (On That Day) and consider the aesthetic, *midrashic* difference of this alternative.

Play recorded example #18—*Bayom Hahu* sung by Cantor Faith Steinsnyder

Another reason why the child-like traditional **Bayom Hahu** will probably remain in place is its position in the service's progression. There is a psychological time shift that occurs after the conclusion of the *Amidah* (the seventeen blessings silently articulated while standing). From being "present" in our devotion, our minds shift first to the past for the *Kaddish* (the memorial sanctification of God's name) and, then, to the future, the conclusion of the service and the *Kiddush* (blessing of the wine and social hour after services). Our *kavannah*, the clarity of our informed intention, loses focus.

This is also why there is no opportunity in our present service structure for a *midrashic* setting of the great, poetic hymn *Adon Olam.*

The hymn's author, thought to be Solomon ibn Gabirol (1021-1058), the Sephardic poet philosopher, who lived in Malaga, Spain. *Adon Olam* consists of ten lines. The first six express the cosmic concept of God, and the final four explore the inner space of a person of faith and the ultimate trust that God engenders. The last words of the hymn, "*Adonai* is with me, I shall not fear," are taken from Psalm 118:6, one of the passages of Hallel. *Adon Olam* is used as a concluding hymn and begins the daily morning service.

The name *Adon* recalls the biblical patriarch Abraham, the first one to address God with this title (Bereishit 15:2; Eitz Yosef), and the one who instituted the morning prayers (Berachot 26b) (Vilna Gaon).

Even poems known to us primarily as hymns need *mazal* (luck) to be in the right place at the right time to be set and accompanied by appropriate *midrashic* music. From a musical point of view *Adon Olam* is hardly ever set correctly.

This is mainly due to its position at the very beginning of the weekday morning service, when no one has time to spend singing it, or at the very conclusion of Shabbat and Festival services, when it tends to be dismissed as a catchy, repetitive tune with little or no regard for the full import of the words. By the end of services, people's minds are on the upcoming *Motzi* (Blessing of the Bread) and *Kiddush* (Blessing of the Wine) that follows, and not on spending time to really make a connection between the text and its reflective musical setting.

It is like viewing great art from a passing train when one is impatient, weary, or hungry. The timing is unfortunate and hardly favorable for a real appreciation. Conducive times and places within worship are necessary for musical settings to be properly created, performed, and comprehended.

Even though it is detached from all the thematic material that precedes it, Ernest Bloch's great setting of *Adon Olam* at the conclusion of his *Avodas Hakodesh* (Sacred Service) remains singularly special and spiritual. It takes a concert setting, where we are not rushing to another experience, to savor its setting. Each stanza's idea is set to individual, different music, that carefully word paints, creates a compelling dramatic mood, and above all, develops its musical energies with each idea, as opposed to employing a repetitive, strophic setting (a recurring melody).

Consider the dichotomy of *Adon Olam* as a magnificent expression of an infinite cosmic deity while, simultaneously, the still small voice within us all.

Adon Olam, asher malach b'terem koly'tzir niv'ra,

l'eit na'asah v'cheftzo kol, azai melech sh'mo nikra.

> You are the Eternal God, who reigned before any being had
> been created; when all was done according to Your will, al-
> ready then You were Sovereign.

V'acharei kich'lot hakol, l'vado yimloch nora;

v'hu hayah, v'hu hoveh, v'hu yih'yeh b'tif'arah.

> And after all has ceased to be, still You reign in solitary majesty;
> You were, You are, You will be in glory.

V'hu echad, v'ein sheini l'hamshil lo, l'hach'bira,

bli reisheet, b'li tach'lit, v'lo ha'oz v'hamis'ra

> And You are One; none other can compare to You, or consort
> with You; You are without beginning, without end; You alone
> are power and dominion.

V'hu Eili, v'chai go'ali, v'tzir chev'li v'eit tzara,

V'hu nisi umanos li, m'nat kosi b'yom ek'ra.

> And You are my God, my living Redeemer, my Rock in time
> of trouble an distress; You are my banner and my refuge, my
> benefactor when I call on You.

B'yado af'kid ruchi, b'eit ishan v'aira,

V'im ruchi g'viyati, Adonai li, v'lo ira.

> Into Your hands I entrust my spirit, when I sleep and when I
> wake;
>
> and with my spirit, my body also: You are with me, I shall not
> fear.

We simply miss all these nuanced gradations of belief in our strophic musical settings. The repetition discounts the vastness and elegance of the poem.

I urge the reader to listen to Ernest Bloch's setting as well as evocative settings by Lukas Foss and by Mordechai Seter, the Israeli composer.

•

At this point, I offer a through-composed setting of my own that includes a strophic returning melody as well, for those listeners who need a recurring melody to hold on to. Both previous settings of mine were commissioned as entirely strophic settings. This recent effort, composed as a birthday tribute to my dear teacher and friend Samuel Adler, seeks to combine both the intellectual, "left-brained" through-composed strategy with a melodic "life-line" that returns in various ways.

Play # 19—*Adon Olam* for SATB Chorus, by the Westminster Conservatory Youth Chorale conducted by Dr. Frank Abrahams

In setting music for liturgy, there is another reason for offering a *midrashic* musical approach. Though there are times when existing folk musical settings are fine for communal usage, at special times we benefit from a dramatic "Theatre-of-the-Spirit" approach. Here is an example of where there is a mix of both approaches. During the High Holydays we sing *Avinu Malkeinu* (Our Parent, Our King) several times.

The final verse attributed to Rabbi Akiva, is most often used in the traditional folk version. It reads:

Avinu Malkeinu, chaneinu v'aneinu, ki ein banu ma'asim.

Our Parent, Our Sovereign hear our voice and answer us.

Assei imanu ts'dakah vachesed, vehoshieinu.

Have pity and be compassionate on us, and accept our prayer.

In recorded example #18 the text is first heard as an original, folk-like melody, sung *a capella* (without accompaniment). It is then re-stated in a choral harmonization, and then sung a third time in counterpoint by both the cantor and the choir.

Play recorded example #20—*Avinu Malkeinu,* sung by Hazzan Nathan Lam.

This musical treatment follows one *keva* of introducing counterpoint while also creating a *midrash* on how we pray. Sometimes we pray by ourselves in the quiet simplicity of our hearts, and sometimes we are part of a congregation in a more sophisticated concerted voice. However, there are times of deep emotion, when we beseech God to hear our deepest longings, where our individual yearning rises above the communal plea. We are both part of a *kehilla* (a community) and alone in our deficiencies and weaknesses. It is a most emotional experience and one that is dramatically appropriate for this *Yamim Noraim* (Days of Awe) text setting.

•

A final consideration in this chapter on musical settings of the liturgy must be the understanding of Hebrew as a language.

Although, in our prayer books we have translations included beneath, or on opposing pages accompanying texts, saying and listening to the aural impact of the language is of primary importance. With the growing numbers of Jewish worshippers who cannot pronounce, read, or understand Hebrew, both literary and musical challenges present themselves for revolutionary change. This is what Heschel means when he talks about revolution. However, we are now in a time when our prayer experience is often clouded by musical smokescreens, frantic diversions suggesting facile feelings of ecstasy that are too often mistaken for honest prayer. It amounts to change for change's sake.

New modes of American Jewish prayer that balance tradition with innovative alternatives need not be ersatz Gospel, New Age, Evangelical, or second-hand Christian worship at all. Jewish tradition has given us all the musical materials we need to move forward with integrity and quiet assuredness in adapting to our future needs. The key is always awareness and understanding of the past (both its strengths and weaknesses) and an organic development of the present that considers less sensational quick fixes.

Aside from teaching the congregation to read and understand Hebrew, there are two contemporary musical solutions. The first is to incorporate English translations within the setting of the Hebrew as in the recorded example of #21 -- *L'dor Vador* (In Every Generation).

Play recorded example # 21—*L'dor Vador*, sung by Cantor Jay Frailich and chorus.

The other is to set the full prayer in English, as in illustration #19— the Rosh Hashanah cantor's plea for the congregation *Hin'ni*. For many, this setting will be the first time that the true meaning of *Hin'ni* will be heard and considered.

Play musical example #22—*Hin'ni* sung by Cantor Faith Steinsnyder.

While these are newer, less explored and developed musical alternatives, they are pragmatic approaches born out of the modern congregant's inability to read and understand complete settings in Hebrew. New English composed settings, under skillful hands, may truly bring American Jews to a refreshed level of understanding in the "revolutionary"modern worship service. It is entirely dependent upon the quality of creative musical invention that is brought to play through this necessity and, of course, the future musical and literary literacy of American Jewry.

•

Chapter 12
The *Midrash* of Life Cycle Music

Hope is like peace. It is not a gift from God.

It is a gift only we can give one another.

— *Elie Wiesel*

Realizing a fulfilling life as a Jew is far more than identifying and praying to God. It is also being mindful, hopeful, and active in Jewish life in all of its stages. In *Pirkei Avot* (Ethics of Our Ancestors) it is noted that the world stands on three foundations: *Al haTorah,* on the study of Torah; *al haAvodah,* on worship (or sacred labor) *v'al g'milut chasadim,* on the performance of just and moral deeds. To remind ourselves of these values we have created periodic milestone rituals of commemoration, collectively called Jewish life cycle events. Beginning with birth and continuing even after death, we pause along each cadence in the journey to give thanks to God for the gift of our own and others' lives, the opportunity to involve ourselves in all of life's joys and sorrows, and most importantly, to reassess where we are in life's progress. Though there are many life cycle ritual subdivisions, for our musical purposes these events may be classified in four general areas: baby naming, *Bar and Bat Mitzvah*, *Chatunah* (wedding), *and Levayat Hameit* (accompanying deceased and consoling the bereaved) including *Yizkor* (regularly remembering those who have passed on). A significant body of music has developed throughout our history that addresses each of these commemorations. The best musical settings use *midrashic* techniques that we have discussed to provide historic illumination, perspective, context, and hope for the future.

Demonstrating the simultaneity of time, *midrashic* music has the ability to set the event in historic perspective, while placing the focus in an informed Jewish presence and projecting the recipient, the attending company, and the spirit of the event into the future.

The music reminds us of who we were as a people, what we stand for as individuals today, and all that we aspire to become as an ethical and moral force in the years ahead; the three simultaneous time frames discussed previously.

Composing a new work for a life cycle event is always an interesting venture. Because it is usually associated with an impending event, the desires of ancillary personalities other than the central subject often come into play. These side issues bring color to our focus of the question, "What considerations make creating music for a specific life cycle occasion distinct from other Jewish musical compositions?"

The answer for me has always been in understanding the subtext of a life cycle commemoration. What does this event mean in emotional terms not only to the celebrant but also to all the participants? As an example, if an effective wedding service is written for an approaching marriage, even though the purpose of a wedding march is clear, or the text of the *Sheva B'rachot* (Seven Wedding Blessings) is specifically mandated, there is a menu of possible sub-texts in the relationships of relatives and friends of the bride and groom the composer can draw upon to give deeper resonance and *midrash* to the *pshat* immediacy of the text or activity.

One of the intriguing aspects to this particular tailoring of music for a specific occasion is that, if the composer conceives of it in a knowing fashion, the music often takes on universal proportions that were hardly imagined at the outset.

Baby naming, or songs sung at a *brit milah* (circumcision), are all about past traditions of people-hood, tribal solidarity, the newborn's innocent, pure presence, and bright future, hopes, and aspirations for the child. All provide subtexts.

Musical examples # 11 and #12, *B'ni and Biti,* in chapter ten have illustrated a dramatic approach. Here they are good examples of focusing in on the creative subtext and universality. Simultaneously, these are the sons and daughters that our parents wanted us to be, the idealized way we think of our children, and hope that in the future these values will be passed along to their children as well.

There is an additional pragmatic production issue to consider. Unless an *Erev Shabbat* service in temple enables instruments, and or a choir to join the cantor in presenting the music, musical accompaniments need to be minimal. Most of baby-naming celebrations, in fact, are done in the home. Consequently, apart from an *a cappella* song, or one accompanied by guitar or keyboard, the alternative is using a pre-recorded accompaniment on a CD player while the cantor or performer sings to it. If realized correctly, this newer way of accompanying can be quite effective musically.

In creating celebratory music for a bar or bat mitzvah, there are several approaches that are available to the *midrashic* composer. The first is to create a musical image of the child as a pure reflection of God's spirit. I took this approach when I created a setting of a prayer found in *Shacharit* (the daily morning prayers) *Nishama Shenatata Bi, - The Soul You Have Given me is a Pure One.* Lowell and Sandy Milken commissioned this setting in honor of the Bar Mitzvah of their son, Jeremy.

Play example #23—*Nishama Shenatata Bi*, sung by Cantor Faith Steinsnyder.

A second approach is to create a musical *drash* of the particular *Torah* and/or *Haftarah* portion of the bar or bat mitzvah that reflects the child's affinities and values.

For Morgan Fine's bar mitzvah his Torah portion was *Bamidbar* (*In the Desert*). Morgan's family asked if I would combine his love of music (a flute solo and obbligato) and his love of animals (the theme of the *Haftarah* portion) in this musical *drash*, entitled *The Covenant* with a versatile text by lyricist Marcia Hain Engle.

Play example # 24—*The Covenant* narrated by Rabbi Morley Feinstein and sung by Cantor Jay Frailich.

A third approach is to create a *drash* that honors the *bar* or *bat mitzvah* and in some manner comments, reflects, or pays tribute to the family's history of activities and affiliations. When Ricky and Madelyn Mishkin Katz's daughter, Amy, was to become bat mitzvah during Shabbat *Parashat* (Torah portion) *Lech L'chah*, they asked me to compose a song that Madelyn's brother, Doug Mishkin, a well-known camp song leader and folk artist, might perform following the Torah service. Doug and I had worked together at the National Federation of Temple Youth's Kutz Camp and I was quite familiar with his voice and style of singing.

So in effect, the resulting *S'i Na Einayich* with a lyric by Marcia Hain Engle reflected not only the Torah portion *Lech L'cha* and the implication of Amy's (and all Jews') rite of passage and unique search towards a Godly direction in life's journey, but, by its style, guitar instrumentation, and musical vocabulary, also acknowledged the influence of her family and camping experience upon her growth and love of Judaism as well.

Play example #25 — *S'i Na Einayich*, sung by Cantor Wally Shachet-Briskin.

In creating music for the Jewish wedding, the skillful composer considers these possibilities among the personality dynamics of the wedding participants:

The bride – Idealized love, fulfilled fairy tale, romance, purity, center of admiration, and love of her groom, separation from parents, new happy life with husband, issues of balance in new relationship, etc.

The groom – Fulfillment of quest, idealized union, romance, rite of passage into manhood, anxiety of new role, willingness to please his bride, separation from parents and former female relationships, etc.

The parents of the bride and groom – Moment of fulfillment for children's happiness, proper dignity, saying good-bye to their children and their own youth, a possible empty nest, validating prestige and position in peer community, confronting and welcoming the inevitabilities of the future, saying an optimistic hello to an extended family with high hopes for their children's happiness.

I once received a commission by a father of two daughters, after his younger daughter celebrated her marriage, to create a wedding service for the older daughter who had not, as yet, even met her future husband. The *Sheva B'rachot* from that service *Kol Simcha* (included here as musical example #3 from chapter three) must have done its job well. A marriage eventually occurred, the musical wedding service was employed, and the daughter and son-in-law subsequently gave their parents grandchildren.

Many of these psychological dynamics have more to do with the past or future than the present occasion of the marriage. Yet, as noted previously, a meaningful Jewish life (and the creation of life cycle music) is lived simultaneously in all three time frames.

Aside from setting the mood for the occasion, properly setting the accompanying Hebrew and Aramaic texts, providing a unique new artistic work that punctuates, reflects, projects, and elevates the moment, the Jewish music composer must also be sensitive to the dynamics of all the participants by building in metaphoric musical elements that will gratify the needs and desires of those celebrants and ancillary figures in the life cycle music.

A cantor can add great color (or a telling comment) to a life cycle event by selecting and matching the right music with the right celebrant.

A friend of mine who is a cantor tells a hilarious story of a bride who was such a *meeskeit* (Yiddish for homely) and her parents were such *farbissoners* (whining cranks) that, when it came time for him to chant the *Sheva B'rachot* during the wedding ceremony, he looked into the bride's face, and then towards the parents' frowns, and felt the compulsion to sing the seven blessings not to the usual wedding music, but to the cantillation for *Eicha* (Lamentations and mourning sung on *Tisha B'Av*, [the ninth day of Av commemorating several tragedies in Jewish history]). As a professional, he, of course, resisted the urge.

From a composer's point of view, these occasions are also wonderful opportunities for exploring artistic ground that has not been previously traversed. I remember learning that when Shakespeare wrote *Romeo and Juliet*, the Jewish community in England had long been in exile. Even the character of Shylock in *The Merchant of Venice* was derived from literary stereotypes that Marlowe and others portrayed, and not from Shakespeare's first-hand observations of English Jewry.

This led me to an artistic supposition that I, as a Jewish composer privileged to be living in the 20th and 21st centuries, might, on occasion, compose Jewish music in a style that could not have been created in former times. Provincial Jewish ghetto life precluded an awareness and facility of other cosmopolitan musical idioms and styles. In effect, I could create a pseudo-historic musical past that was, in reality, impossible to us at the time. It might be considered a musical *tikkun olam.* On one occasion I decided to compose an orthodox Jewish wedding service in the Elizabethan style that might have been employed if Shakespeare's Romeo and Juliet, surely the model for the most profound lovers, were Jewish.

This may sound like an odd flight of fancy, but artists create mental possibility data files all the time. They can then draw from and reshuffle them during the creative process. Remember, nothing comes from nothing. The result of this blueprint was a wedding service entitled *Kol Sason* scored for cantor, recorder, keyboard (harpsichord or organ), viola, and light percussion.

It was composed in honor of the wedding of Madelyn Pullman to Martin Schloss. I liked it so much that, a few years later, Cantor Stephen Richards performed *Kol Sason* at my own wedding to Susan. Listen to the *Sheva B'rachot* from *Kol Sason* as Romeo and Juliet (if they were Jewish) might have experienced them.

Play example #26—*Sheva B'rachot*, sung by Hazzan Chayim Frenkel.

The last category is music for remembering the deceased and consoling the bereaved. It is perhaps the most interesting to compose.

At its most effective, this music surpasses the *pshat* approach and never punctuates a sad occasion with simply sad music. The result would be melodramatic and, I believe, demeaning to the deceased's memory.

I go one step further than Solomon Ibn Gabirol's philosophy of death in his *Mibhar HaPeninim*: *"Look upon death with indifference, for its bitterness is commensurate with its fear"*.

I underscore death as a divine release from life's bitterness and a state of perfection to be accepted with understanding and grace. This philosophy produces *midrashic* music of consolation.

Another approach might be to emphasize the perfection and peacefulness of the *Olam Haba* (*The World to Come*) and God's ultimate wisdom and understanding in calling us all to return at the correct moment in God's time.

Example #25 - is a setting of *This Quiet Dust* by John Hall Wheelock. Consider how these words as *midrash* are both wise and comforting.

Here in my curving arms I cup this quiet dust;
I lift it up. Here is the mother of all thought;
Of this the shining heavens are wrought.
The laughing lips, the feet that rove,
The face, the body that you love;
Mere dust, no more, yet nothing less.
And this has suffered consciousness,
Passion and terror, this again shall suffer
Passion, death, and pain. For as all flesh must die,
So all, now dust, shall live; 'tis natural.
Yet hardly do I understand - here, in the hollow of my hand
A bit of God I keep, between two vigils fallen asleep.

Play recorded example #27—*This Quiet Dust,* sung by Cantor Faith Steinsnyder.

Another approach is to set a scriptural psalm text from the *Yizkor* service in a way that, though the word image might be a sad one, the *midrashic* musical approach in a gentle, lyrical way comforts us by reminding the mourner, and reemphasizing the natural, organic order of the world. This encourages consolation in the anticipation of the ensuing life eternal.

Enosh (Psalm 103:15-17) Memorial Liturgy

Enosh kechatsir yamav, K'tsits hasadeh kein yatsits.

Our days are like grass we shoot up like flowers that fade

Ki ruach avrabo v'einenu, v'lo yakirenu od mimkomo.

And die as the chill wind passes over them.

V'chesed Adonai meiolam v'ad olam al y'reiav

Yet, Your love for those who revere You is everlasting.

V'tsidkato livnei vanim.

Your righteousness extends to all generations.

Play recorded example # 28—*Enosh,* sung by Cantor Faith Steinsnyder.

It is helpful when composing or listening to life cycle music to focus in on the dramatic potential of the moment by asking these questions as you import the musical message:

1. Does the music have a larger than life conception?

2. Does it present a point of view that is fresh?

3. Is its musical idea clearly stated in its first moments?

4. Are there built-in reminders, as repetition in its structure, so that thematic importance can be recalled and processed?

5. Does it possess an attractive musical subject that we can employ, empathize with and root for its successful fulfillment?

6. Is the subtext clear as it underscores the text?

7. Does it use dramatic opposition to access a compelling, *midrashic* interpretation?

•

Chapter 13
The *Midrash* of Wisdom Music

In seeking wisdom the first step is silence, the second: listening, the third: remembering, the fourth: practicing, the fifth: teaching others.

—Solomon Ibn Gabirol

Seeking wisdom through music in our time is, indeed, as challenging as it was in the 11th century for Spanish scholar Solomon Ben Judah. Known to us as Ibn Gabirol, his first recommendation to us in our quest for wisdom is silence. Do we have enough quiet times in our cacophonous lives these days to find adequate moments of meditative silence? Our lives are so filled with ourselves and the latest chatter that we often do not let God in. In the raucous din of ecstatic, participatory, worship music, where are the quiet moments needed to hear God's still, small voice, and thoughtfully take in the prayerful message it offers?

Ibn Gabirol next recommends listening. Not just hearing, but active, focused listening of what is being communicated. As mentioned previously, because of all the sonic information being catapulted towards us today we have learned to be skillful about blocking out active listening and letting sounds go through us like elevator music. Though we hear more words and music around us than ever before, the art of active listening has been impeded in this generation by the sheer bulk of sound that surrounds us.

An outgrowth of true, active listening, especially in regard to understanding both spiritual and musical ideas, is remembering. It has been pointed out that the physicality of music exists only one nanosecond at a time. We create the gestalt in our memory. By remembering and stringing these sound mosaics together with musical logic, we create a linear entity in our minds where none actually exists in real time. If we cannot remember the details of what we listen to, then how are we to make accurate associative meanings of the larger mosaic?

Ibn Gabirol's fourth step, practicing what was actively heard, is also encouraged by the act of remembering. Are we teaching our children how to actively listen and remember? Memorization seems to have been dismissed with one push of a computer key. Multiplication tables are no longer memorized, because we now have calculators. Spelling isn't memorized, because we have spell check, and poems and monologues are not memorized because we can rely on Google for a précis.

Are we practicing and teaching our children aural practice skills in enlightened music appreciation courses in our schools? Sadly, music is always the first subject to suffer budget cuts and programming limitations in both public and private elementary and high schools. Jewish day schools may practice singing; but do they practice active listening?

We have more information than ever before in our computers. But has that data been digested by our affective and cognitive memory to become part of our inner, personal, integrated data bank—those developed connections that open us up to inspiration, greatness, gratitude, and a consistency of God in our lives? This inner data bank that has experienced, remembered, and appreciated greatness and beauty is sometimes referred to as "taste."

Adhering to Ibn Gabirol's prescription for seeking wisdom becomes increasingly more difficult as we abrogate our personal inner responsibility for its search by assigning surrogate power to mechanical forces outside of us.

Ibn Gabirol's final step—teaching others—only works effectively when others want and are open to being taught. My first composing teacher, Robert Starer [z"l], once asked me if I knew why Bartok had never written a viola concerto earlier on in his productive career. It was an unfinished work upon his death. I didn't know the answer. He taught me a great verity when he replied, "No one asked him to compose one." There has to be an arena for artists and performers to work in. They cannot practice creating or teaching in a vacuum. We cannot practice listening or learning without a desire for that forum to be built, utilized, and valued. Or, as it is written, "The beginning of wisdom is to acquire wisdom, with all your acquisitions acquire discernment."

Another issue that comes into play when creating "wisdom" music, is that categorizations of truths and wisdom are often as ephemeral as the times, mores, and sources from which these insights and perceptions are culled. Additionally, musical settings of these bits of wisdom are highly subjective, and sometimes, more influential in shaping our belief system than we care to imagine. Tom Stafford, the author of *Mind Hacks*, delineates this problem even further when he describes that:

> Perception is a fundamentally under-constrained problem. You get information in through your senses, but not enough information to be absolutely sure of what is causing those sensations. A good example is perception of depth in vision. You get a pattern of light falling on your retinas in two dimensions, and from that you infer a three dimensional world, using various clever calculations of the visual system and some assumptions about what is likely. But because the process remains fundamentally under-constrained, there is always the possibility that you will see something that isn't really there – that is, your visual system will take in a pattern of information and decide that it is more likely to be produced by a scenario different from the real one.

This finite visual acuity is analogous to our experiential limitations when it comes to intellectualizing and canonizing morality and wisdom. This is why we rely on faith in God and the experience of others to guide us along this tenuous path. As Spinoza assesses in his *Ethics*, *"The mind's highest good is the knowledge of God, and the mind's highest virtue is to know God."*

However, in the music of Jewish life, it is our religious and educational leaders who are best trained to understand words and have less experience actively listening to music. With little or no formal education in the subject, they are most often the ones responsible for making the musical policy that guides the selection and emphasis of these wisdom settings. The results for adult audiences are at best charmingly folk-like and, at worst, adolescent, rather silly, musical treatments of profound truths.

For our *midrashic* musical classification, with some exceptions, "wisdom music" generally means those musical settings of brief texts that are culled from scripture (the Torah, Prophets, Psalms, and Scrolls), liturgy (Sabbath, Festival, and High Holiday worship texts), as well as from the *Mishneh* (Oral Law), *Talmud* (the discussion of the *Mishneh*), and rabbinic epigrams by more recent scholars, poets, teachers, and leaders. They are often employed as teaching points at Jewish life cycle events as well as at prayer services.

Because the Jewish educational arena is mostly focused on youth, the simple, didactic quality of these wisdom texts in their conciseness is traditionally comforting and bears the *hechsher* (imprimatur) of wise truth. This growing body of music is frequently used in summer camping, and at pre-school, elementary, and high school levels of Jewish education to teach Jewish values.

In recent times, while not originally part of our modern liturgy, these aphorisms and teachings have become increasingly incorporated and are heard during the worship service for both children and adults as a prelude to prayer, an interim musical meditation, or a concluding anthem. It is hoped that these musical settings become more interesting as the role of the *Hazzan* (cantor) evolves as much to encompass pastoral and teaching arenas as it has liturgically at services. The settings' worth as didactic shorthand have certainly been proven. In all cases, wisdom music, by its conciseness and accessibility, is certain to continue to grow and become increasingly featured on the Jewish musical menu.

The non-specific occasion and function of this music tends to suggest use of melodic ideas that are less codified by *nusach*, cantillation, or *misinai* melodies (anonymous, traditional, identifiable folk motives), and musical sounds less formal, more contemporary in nature, and only slightly "Jewish." When set by lesser-trained songwriters, the amorphous melodic vocabulary sometimes causes these trendy musical settings to range from too casual to downright banal.

An ancillary truth is that the more these brief moments are presented as complete thoughts, the less *zitzfleisch* we will continue to develop as listeners.

Concurrently, the less listening experiences we involve ourselves with that are more slowly but more thoroughly developed, the less actively considered, critical listening faculties we will utilize to as well.

Remember my initial listening anecdote in Chapter One? This is precisely why this short form of imparting Jewish epigrammatic wisdom is becoming so attractive to listeners who are most experienced with processing brief sound bytes. All this being noted, in the hands of knowing composers, these musical "snapshots" can be welcomed additions to the literature.

The knack in composing and choosing a better setting of wisdom music is to understand the age group for which it is intended, and to select *midrashic* approaches that are accessible to the understanding of these groups. The irony here is that many settings once created for pre-school aged youngsters and elementary aged students are now being sung and lauded by adults as *"magnum opera."*

Nevertheless, knowing your audience's initial capabilities and preferences is still practical. As a composer, I have set wisdom texts for ages from pre-schoolers up through adults. The joy in creating this work is in culling the sincerity, belief, innocence, hope, and optimism of these brief sayings and dressing them in a *midrashic* musical garb that adds elevation, importance, and context to the words.

With a brief moment in time and a terse text to set, the effective composer of wisdom music deals in gestures more than developed, spun-out musical constructs. It is very much like composing media music in that you often have a span of a minute or less to communicate a musical idea. What techniques does a composer employ in this case? All the parameters of music that we outlined in Chapter Two come into play except that they are even more vividly introduced. Because there is less time for development, the initial exposure has to be far more memorable in a dramatically impressive way.

For example: a melody might begin with a dramatic interval, or a rhythmic motive that may be particularly alluring. Perhaps, the style of music is obliquely matched with the historicity of the text, or a dissonant harmony might provocatively draw you in. Maybe the dynamic is ultra soft or loud to grab your awareness, or a textural device screams out for your attention. Whatever the device, it must make a gesture that is immediate and summons the audience to listen actively, relate to the text, and encourage them to remember it.

Wisdom music, when it is best utilized, serves as a topic sentence, an object lesson, a *mishneh* for further delineation and discussion. In this way, it makes a good prelude to Torah study or a rabbinic sermon, or as a musical motto for a themed Shabbat service.

This chapter offers to you five graded settings from pre-school to adult, some for school, some for worship, and some for life cycle celebrations, with comments about how and why the dramatic, *midrashic* approach was used, and how this point of view colors each text. This chapter also demonstrates how *midrashic* settings may comment on existing texts, texts that formerly did not exist and were newly created as *midrash*, and even traditional rituals that have no text.

The first is a setting that I composed for young kindergarten and early elementary school students as part of a children's suite entitled *Shirei Avot* (songs from the tractate *Avot—Our Ancestors*). Commissioned by Cantor Jay Frailich for the *Hashirim* Children's Choir of University Synagogue in Los Angeles, the suite deals with manners and proper behavior.

Im Ein Torah (Ein Derech Eretz) In *Pirkei Avot* (sometimes called *Ethics of our Fathers*) 3:21, Rabbi Elazar ben Azariah offers "*Im ein torah ein derech eretz, im ein derech eretz ein torah,*" *Where there is no Torah there is no culture (literally the way to go or behave); and where there is no culture there is no Torah. Where there is no wisdom there is no fear of God, and where there is no fear of God there is no wisdom. Where there is no knowledge there is no discernment; and where there is no discernment there is no knowledge. Where there is no food there is no Torah; and where there is no Torah there is no food.*"

I chose to set it in a simple Mozartian classical style. Classical to me has always meant elegantly clean, balanced lines, and harmony with little or no frills. This was my musical *midrash* on good manners. No affectations, simplicity, and a dearth of affluent materialism. Torah was all a child needed to learn the way.

The music offered the *drash* that the more pure values a child is given and the less material "stuff," the better chance one has of raising well-mannered children—not boring children, remember this is Mozart—but children who understand the balance of a community standard and their proper place within that spectrum.

Play recorded CD# 29—*Im Ein Torah,* sung by Hazzan Nathan Lam and the children of Stephen S. Wise Temple.

V'sham'ru / When You Keep the Sabbath

There are at least two parts to *midrash* that need to be addressed: the **text** and the interpretive ***midrash.*** Most of this book develops how a composer brings musical tools to the interpretive task. However, it has been assumed that the text itself was understood on a basic level. Beside a good English translation, it did not need additional texts to explain it. Unfortunately, as this is written, many Jewish worshippers today do not understand Hebrew and the nuances of the language.

These are the texts, especially in the Shabbat service, that might well benefit from *midrashic* addenda that can be bonded to them, forming a larger construct in a sacred service. We might call this category a hyphenate: one in that it is neither wholly liturgical, nor an independent wisdom text, but a synthesis of both.

In this setting of the *V'sham'ru* commissioned by Cantor Philip Goldstein of Congregation Ner Tamid of Henderson, Nevada, I begin with a free chant setting of the *V'sham'ru* prayer in Hebrew. One could possibly chant it alone and move on in the service. However, I perceived it as both a liturgical entity and a *mishneh* for a musical discussion or *midrash*. As the reason for celebrating the Shabbat is so central to a Shabbat service, I felt this hyphenate text could serve effectively as a topic for musical meditation and discussion. This is a new direction in synagogue music. Once implied by the performance of a skilled Hazzan, the nuance of the *V'sham'ru*'s terse primary text might well benefit from a bit more exposition, both in literary terms and in its contemporary musical interpretation.

I have always admired Achad Haam's aphorism, "As much as Israel has kept the Sabbath, the Sabbath has kept Israel." Asher Ginzberg (1856 – 1927), a Ukranian Jew born near Kiev, assumed the Hebrew *nom de plume* Achad Haam (One of the People) as he wrote and became active in early Zionism. Later, he was a thoughtful critic of Theodore Herzl's work with the World Zionist Organization. Their difference was whether land ownership was inextricably allied with spiritual ownership. Achad Haam felt that people-hood was just as much about language, rituals, and shared wisdom.

As I often do when conceiving the architecture for a new musical worship service, I called upon one of my lyric collaborators, Marcia Hain Engle, to paraphrase and expand on a wisdom text, in this case, Achad Haam's saying. After our lively e-mail study sessions of the saying's possibilities, Ms. Hain Engle's knowing lyric provided an additional wisdom text from which to create the larger construct. Here is the final text.

V'sham'ru / **When You Keep the Sabbath**

Erev Shabbat Liturgy, English Lyric by Marcia Hain Engle,
Based on Achad Haam.   Music by Michael Isaacson.

Unaccompanied cantorial chant
*V'sham'ru v'nei Yisrael et ha-Shabbat laasot et ha-Shabbat l'dorotam b'rit
olam beini uvein b'nei Yisrael ot hi l'o-lam, ki sheishet yamim asah Adonai
et hashamayim v'et haaretz uvayom hash'vi-i shavat vayinafash.*

Unison Choir
When you keep the Sabbath, the Sabbath will keep you.
With joyfulness, in holiness, to rest and to renew.
When you keep the Sabbath, the Sabbath will keep you.
V'sham'ru, v'sham'ru, et ha-Shabbat, ha-Shabbat.

Duet
Resting from our labors for all those precious hours,
Taking time to share with God the earth, the sun, the flowers,
Reflecting to sustain our core and discovering anew that

Unison Choir with Cantor and Congregation
When you keep the Sabbath, the Sabbath will keep you.
With joyfulness, in holiness, to rest and to renew.
When you keep the Sabbath, the Sabbath will keep you.
V'sham'ru, v'sham'ru, et ha-Shabbat, ha-Shabbat.

Duet
No matter where we found ourselves, our covenant with God
Reminded us to reach the heights beyond what we could see,
To light the lights, begin anew, and set our spirits free for

Unison Choir with Cantor and Congregation
When you keep the Sabbath, the Sabbath will keep you.
With joyfulness, in holiness, to rest and to renew.
When you keep the Sabbath, the Sabbath will keep you.
  V'sham'ru, v'sham'ru, et ha-Shabbat, ha-Shabbat.
  V'sham'ru, v'sham'ru, et ha-Shabbat, ha-Shabbat.

Play CD# 30—V'sham'ru / When You Keep the Sabbath, sung by Cantor Phillip Goldstein.

Circles – A Wedding Song

Sometimes a silent Jewish ritual, without a primary text attached to it, calls for *midrashic* music to clarify its purpose and offer a poetic overlay to the physical action. This is the case with the marriage ritual of the bride's circling the groom seven times immediately after reaching the altar. Traditionally, the seven circles have several meanings. One biblical interpretation suggests that, just as Joshua encircled the city of Jericho to bring down its walls, the bride encircles the groom to break down any walls or barriers between them. (A nice bit of *midrash* in itself.)

Another prophetic meaning, which I incorporated in this music, comes from Hosea 2:21,22, enumerating seven expressions of wedded unity between God, the bride and the groom: *"I will betroth thee unto Me **forever**. I will betroth thee unto Me **in mercy**, and **in judgment**, and **in loving kindness**, and **in righteousness**: I will betroth thee unto me **in faithfulness**, and **you shall know God**."*

A beautiful Hassidic explanation suggests that the seven circles represent the seven orders of nature, including time, week of seven days; space, seven spiritual heavens; and being, seven emotional attributes; indicating the bride's investment in the marriage by an absolute commitment.

At contemporary weddings, with an awareness of feminism and egalitarianism added to the ritual texture, the bride sometimes circles the groom three times, the groom circles the bride three times, and they circle together as a couple for the ultimate revolution.

When I was commissioned by Dr. Avrum and Cantor Donna Goldstein to create a song for their daughter Diane Shapiro's marriage to Seth Fersko, I called again on my wonderful lyricist, Marcia Hain Engle, to help me voice a lyric that would add a poetic moment to this silent choreography.   Here is the beautiful text that Ms. Hain Engle provided:

Circles – A Wedding Song

She circles her beloved creating a sacred space
A circle for their family protected by God's grace.

A shelter and a haven for their new married life
Where they will live together as husband and wife.

(Hosea) - V'eirastich Li l'olam b'tzedek, uv'mishpat, uv'chesed,
uv'rachamim

He circles his beloved and the light in his eyes,
Shows no ending, no beginning, or where tomorrow lies.

In joining hands together they see now at a glance,
Eternity, forever, and the future of romance;
they circle as one.

It was set musically as a graceful, slow adagio, a dance of loving commitment. A minor second melodic motif *midrashically* reiterated the unending, faithful, regularity of the wedding ring's endless circle. The piece has continued live on and become a lyrical moment at recent weddings.

Play recorded CD #31—*Circles*, sung by Cantor Patti Linsky.

Biti – My Daughter

I have had the privilege of living during a revolutionary, and stimulating time for women in Judaism. The quest for gender equality within Judaism is particularly evidenced in the early twentieth century. The noted Reconstructionist Rabbi Mordechai Kaplan first introduced the ritual of *Bat Mitzvah* in America on March 18, 1922, as a way of bringing women more equitably into modern Jewish life. The first *Bat Mitzvah* was his daughter, Judith, who later became Judith Kaplan Eisenstein, a distinguished Jewish music educator and musicologist.

Even so, over fifty years later, when I went about composing a song for Jewish daughters that could be sung at a girl's baby naming or at a *Bat Mitzvah*, it was a challenge to find traditional texts to set for these occasions. There were a plethora of texts about *B'ni - my son*. After the obligatory *Eishet Chayil* (Woman of Valor) poem, really more a catalog list of a mother and a wife's duties as a servant than helpful for an independent daughter of Zion, appropriate texts for young women were almost non-existent.

Once more, necessity became the mother of invention. As I could not find existing words to fit a contemporary Jewish life cycle event, a new text was created. I enlisted the talents of Rabbi Kerry Baker, who wrote Hebrew words that sounded scriptural, and reflected modern familial hopes and values assigned to these contemporary occasions. I call your attention to Chapter Ten, where I cite Rabbi Kerry Baker's text. In this case the *midrashic* text that was created became the primary source, as no other primary texts could be found. To contrast the scripture-like text, melodically I chose a downward interval of a major seventh to emphasize the modern, contemporary aspect of this woman being lauded. It was expertly recorded by Cantor Faith Steinsnyder on a CD entitled *Made in America – The Music of Michael Isaacson*.

CD#12 —*Biti* (see Chapter 10 for the text)

My Dear and Treasured Child

Another example of Jewish womens' new equality and, indeed, super-equality is the rather extreme situation where a woman is about to give birth to a child, not by her husband, but by artificial insemination. This is certainly the cutting edge of 21st century technology. I was commissioned by the single mother's parents to create a baby-naming moment for their daughter and her baby. Obviously, it would have been indelicate to mention any masculine reference. The naming was to occur in a temple as a Jewish life cycle response, officiated by the rabbi and cantor. This was, indeed, an interesting assignment. Here's the text that Marcia Hain Engle and I came up with:

I often think I knew you long before you came to be,
I felt your tender presence, and I heard you call to me,
I waited for a long time but I did not wait alone,
We waited for each other, and now you have come home.

Siman tov umazal tov, Siman tov umazal tov
Y'hei lanu uv'kol yisrael, Siman tov umazal tov

My own, my precious baby, my dear and treasured child,
A miracle a gift from God, I feel the heavens smile,
Finally you've arrived, my child, I knew you were so near,
I name you in God's presence, at last, my child, you're here!

With this sign of good fortune and good luck
With this sign of good fortune and good luck
Let us all celebrate God's goodness in our lives
With this sign of good fortune and good luck

Welcome, little angel, let us fill your world with light,
Simon tov, and *mazal tov,* the future's warm and bright,
Welcome little angel, sings the chorus from above,
We will wrap you in a tapestry woven by God's love!

When you hear the musical setting of these words you might very well detect a bitter sweetness in its musical sub-textural approach. Knowing what circumstances and pressures in her life must have convinced this woman to go it alone as a single parent, and what challenges she will face as a single parent raising this child, the music could not help but infuse empathetic, compassionate harmonies, and a tinge of sadness within the melodic love song and the comforting lullaby that it is. I recently learned that the mother sings this to her baby each night as he falls asleep. How grateful I feel to have been asked to be part of the creation of this moment for the mother and child. We wish her and her beautiful child all God's help, the community's love and support and *siman tov umazal tov* (a good sign and the best of luck) in this—life's greatest commitment.

Play recorded CD #32—*My Dear and Treasured Child,* sung by Cantor Patti Linsky.

Acharei Moti - After My Death

Traditionally, music of consolation is only heard in synagogue at Yizkor (Memorial) services during the *Shalosh R'galim* (Three Festivals - Sukkot, Pesach, and Shavuot), and at the afternoon *Yom Kippur* memorial service. Music, other than the Hazzan's chanting of *Eil Malei Rachamim* (God, Filled with Compassion) is proscribed from the funeral service, because it would cause a distraction from mourning the dead.

However, today many reform (and even conservative) mourners choose to add an extra layer of meaning to the funeral service at the chapel before interment by including a song or instrumental preludes and postludes.

Regrettably, many of these musical selections are ill-chosen, inappropriate, and are devoid of Jewish content. In a misguided attempt to cheer up the mourners, the use of pop songs and happy, carefree lyrics seems to discount the pain of bereavement and to cheapen the dignity of the sacred moment. In a misguided effort to lessen the sadness of death, grotesquely unsuitable music is too often employed.

The music still has to maintain the dignity and solemnity of the occasion in comforting the bereaved and not making light of their loss in any way. There are several approaches to achieving this *midrashic* balance. One is to mourn the loss in a dramatic opposite: an affect of celebrating a life well lived, reminding us of our blessings in knowing this person, and all the good the deceased accomplished in life. This dramatic juxtaposition is highly touching without being too cloying or saccharine. This is why I've devoted a significant portion of this aspect of my life cycle music to providing the musical literature with new musical settings of wisdom texts of stature and Jewish significance. *Acharei Moti* is one example. Set in the original Hebrew, it is a musical setting of the first part of a poem by Chaim Nachman Bialik.

Note that the musical setting is more lyrical than dark. Set as a delicate, bittersweet waltz, it sings the tune of the man's life, not the silence of his death. However, the accompaniment is spare and fragile, reminding us that our life's song is not an eternal one and may end any moment in mid-phrase. The transliteration and line translation of Bialik's poem follows:

Acharei moti sifdu kacha li

After my death, thus shall you mourn for me

hayah ish ur'u einenu od.

Say "There was a man - and behold he is no more.

kodem z'mano meit haish hazeh

Before his time did this man die

v'shirat chayav baemtsa nifs'kah.

And the song of his life was interrupted in the middle.

V'tsar od mizmor echad hayah lo;

And what a pity, he had yet one more song;

v'hinei avad hamizmor laad.

And now that song is lost forever."

How sad, he had a lute, a living, feeling soul and when he plucked its strings all the secrets of his heart did he reveal and with all its strings did he speak. But yet one more secret was hidden. With haste did his hands pluck yet one more melody remained within and remains unrevealed till today; and great, very great is the hurt.

(second stanza of poem – unset)

There was a man, and behold, he is no more – the song of his life was interrupted in the middle. One more song he had within himself and now that song is lost, lost forever.

The music creates a spectral waltz, almost like a Dybbuk (a displaced spirit in Jewish folklore) at a wedding of a deceased lover, not menacing, but gracefully floating within our presence. The middle section becomes a bit more urgent, suggesting the finite fragility of time. The melody then returns to the waltz as if to suggest that, while the life has ended, the songs that were sung remain.

Aside from being a beautiful metaphor for everyone's living worth, Bialik's touching expression was and is a reminder to the Jewish community that, in our times, art and artists define us as much as traditional laws and rabbis defined Jews of former times. The song is a wake up call to my sons' generation to teach great music and art to our children, to embrace it in our homes and houses of worship, and nurture and sustain these artists through requests for new works from them for the community. Bialik expresses the longing of all artists to be equally considered in the ongoing *midrash* of Jewish life.

CD #33 *Acharei Moti*, sung by Cantor Faith Steinsnyder.

Wisdom music, though simple, need not be simplistic. It should at once attract us, touch us, and make us think. Wisdom that is entirely left brained, without empathy or compassion, is a mere crossword puzzle skill. Conversely, wisdom music that excites our emotions without calling us to intellectually consider the merits of the idea's temporal universality, separation, elevation, and inherent *midrash* is less than it could be.

A skilled setting of wisdom texts gives "size" to smaller ideas and adds accessibility to the greater ones.

•

Chapter 14
Listening with *Midrashic* Ears

> That which was given was the same for everybody, but that which was received differed from person to person
>
> —*Rabbi Menachem Mendel of Kotzk*

A member of my congregation once confessed to me that after a busy workday in which he is obliged to make decisions and critical judgments, he looks forward to attending worship services so that he does not have to think. He prefers that Judaism wash over him as automatically as his car goes through a carwash, cleansing him of the frantic agenda and mental pressures of his workweek. I suspect that many of our fellow congregants feel the same way. While they correctly see the Temple as a place of refuge with a built-in opportunity for quietude and soulful meditation, they also subscribe to the notion that thinking could intrude upon feeling, and intellectuality might actually curtail spirituality.

The rabbis throughout our Jewish journey did not share this viewpoint. They believed that thinking and conscious deliberation work in balanced conjunction with meditation, and religious feeling, distinguishing us from lower species and enriching our palette of appreciation for God's goodness. The *siddur* (prayer book) is filled with lists and enumerations of historic, moral, and ethical points to be consciously considered by our brains while we pray with all our hearts. In the weekday morning prayers we have a list of deductive and inductive reasoning to warm up our minds along with our souls to the day's challenges.

Conscious prayer need not be a convoluted mental issue. In his classic book on Hassidic Jewish mysticism, *Likutei Maharan*, Rabbi Nachman of Bratslav teaches:

> It is important to not overcomplicate one's prayers. Just by forcing yourself to concentrate on the simple meaning of the words, you can reach great levels of *kavanah* (intention). The essence of prayer entails straightforward, simple understanding of the words.

In this book's introduction, I outlined the basic process that I go through each time I pre-compose a musical setting of a text for liturgy, life cycle, or even a poem with an independent artistic *midrash*. I start by compiling a list of questions.

What does the text expect of me and what do I expect from the text and my relationship with it? By changing the first person to the third person, an active listener can become more closely involved in the creative process by using the same inquisitive process. Certainly neither difficult nor beyond one's reach, it does require turning off the automatic pilot and paying attention to the moment. While a bit more labor intensive, it is certainly worth the added effort.

Here are my ten introductory questions restated for the active listener:

1. What is the intent and purpose that attracts the composer (or author) to this subject?

2. Is it an emotional or intellectual pull or both?

3. What does it mean in the context of the narrative?

4. What, metaphorically, does it mean to me?

5. What do I need to know about its greater literary and non-literary import?

6. Is there more than one interpretation than my understanding of it?

7. What is the key to making it come alive for me?

8. How does the Hazzan or composer communicate that chosen meaning through music?

9. Is there a musical *midrash* that I can understand in this composition?

10. Does this musical *midrash* touch me?

•

In Chapter One, I advocated active listening through creating expectations. It is only with a finely honed sense of what is possible and should be heard in contrast to what we are actually hearing that we can compare the potential with its realization and maintain a sense of quality in our sacred musical experience. Why would we accept lesser music for our God than we do from music designed for our intelligent entertainment?

Through the progress of this book we have explored more sophisticated issues including the PARDES levels of *midrashic* understanding, the *midrash* of time, positive and negative space, and drama and their individual collective contributions to worship and life cycle music.

With this new information and a keener set of listening skills we can now come closer and more in touch with the text and its musical *midrash* by asking:

1. On what level am I listening to the music in the PARDES garden? Is it straightforward *Pshat* or does it dig deeper to a level of *Remez* or even *Sod*?

2. Where am I in the simultaneity of time? Is this music just for the here and now or does it stimulate a resonance of times

gone by and other bits of once heard Jewish musical sounds and ideas that join the aural mix?

3. Through it do I recall supporting emotions or information from my past that I can bring to this present listening experience? Can I envision a greater realization of its meaning in the future?

4. How does the predominant musical feature of the moment help create an artistic *midrash*? Is there a knowing elegance to the melody? Adventurousness to the harmony? Is the style different than what I hear on A.M. radio?

5. Is the music nuanced by dynamics, texture, and rhythmic accuracy? Does the music ennoble my religious vision of my Judaism or just minimally set the text in an offhand way? Have I experienced matter-of-factness or a revelation?

6. What is the text teaching or expressing? What is the composer's *midrash* of it? Has the composer succeeded in communicating this point of view? Is the composer's or Hazzan's *midrash* confluent with my own?

•

There are many stories about the physical and mental exertion that pious rabbis and Chassidim put into their worship. They hardly let the experience wash innocently over them. They struggled to extract meaning and purpose in every moment of their devotion. We can, as well, by addressing these questions while we listen and participate in prayer.

Perhaps what our congregant who yearned for a spiritual car wash was really saying is that he wanted to transfer from his left brain where the linear logic and reasoning was put on overtime during his workday and give equal time to the right side of his brain; he wanted to dream while awake. This is a valid point of view and should not be discounted. Rabbi Lawrence Kushner continually maintains that the *Tanach* and many rabbinic *midrashim* may be justifiably interpreted as a series of dreams dreamed collectively by our ancestors and handed down to us for our personal, intimately altered, dream state as well.

We do, indeed, come alive in our dreams. The timid are brave, the old are again young, the heavy are slender, the plain looking are beautiful, the dismissed and discounted are loved and valued, and the average thinker shines with superior intellect. All things are possible in our dreams. There is no time or space, no physical or emotional limitations to chain us; we are free to fly on wings of angels.

Every Rosh Hashanah when I hear the *Akeidah*, The Testing of Abraham, I automatically immerse myself in both sides of my brain. While rationally assessing the quality of the cantillation, and the clarity of the chanter's voice, I fall into a dream state, becoming Abraham conflicted by the mandate. I suffer as Sarah is discounted by the silence. I am Isaac confused by the circumstances, and I am the Angel staying the knife in the father's hand and rescuing his son. I am my father, his son, and the father to my own sons. This is the power of the story, the chant, and its annual repetition upon my *midrashic* ears.

Judaism offers us riches if we only dig a bit deeper. To value the Temple sanctuary as merely a place to escape to and not an arena of vital, focused attention is minimizing its ultimate worth. Great issues of good and evil, construct and destruct, and life and death are put before us to both ponder with our minds and embrace with our hearts. To do only one or the other is only to scratch the surface and miss its more profound treasures.

Listening actively to the music and assessing better settings of prayers and texts from the more facile interpretations is our job as well. We are mandated to *Sh'ma*, to listen – not just to the words but also to the music that accompanies them. Just as the words spoken by the rabbi offer us *midrashic* insights, the singing and chanting of the Hazzan also supplies a *midrashic* overlay to heighten both the emotional and the intellectual power of Judaism's profound message and the effectiveness of our worship.

•

I look forward to the time when choral music once again returns to weekly services. It is well worth the personnel investment when one considers the beautiful, *midrashic* musical literature already available by the 19th and 20th century synagogue choral composers. Ultimately, when it comes to synagogue music, I yearn for alertness, an awakening rather than a mindless, robotic ecstasy or, conversely, a fallen lethargy at services.

•

Chapter 15
Afterward

In the world to come they will not ask me, "Why were you not Moses?"
They will ask me, "Why were you not Zusya?"

— *Rabbi Zusya of Hanipoli*

As Rabbi Nachman of Bratslav taught: "All the world is a narrow bridge on which we balance as we fearlessly traverse from one side to the next." The greatest challenge for an artist has always been to communicate the highest individual vision of one's self in a universal way that is accessible to the most diverse audience. The push and pull between the individual and the group, the balance between I and We, is what has always determined the success of an artistic expression. If the artistic vision is too singular, it transcends the sensibilities and faculties of an audience. On the other hand, if it is conceived and produced for the lowest common denominator of perceptions solely to engage or amuse, or even worse, divert the largest audience or congregation, the artistic expression hardly amounts to much more than a momentary pastime.

Professor Yohanan Muffs of the Jewish Theological Seminary points out, in his collection of essays, *Love and Joy*, that this was also the duality of the God of the Torah. The Creator of Creators, the Artist of the World, is a deity who continually seeks to balance being a God of Justice (transcendence) with being an engaging (loving) God. Finding equilibrium between these two dynamics is both God's mission and the essence of the struggle of all those mortals who dare participate in the Godly business of artistic creation.

Today, at the beginning of the 21ˢᵗ century, we are experiencing a striking paradox. With all manner of communication advances on the Internet and recording formats, including CDRs that can be converted into AIFFs or compressed into MP3 sound files to be sent along the digital, on-line network all around the world in seconds, a seductive, explosive mix is being felt, the combination of this technology with the most intense creativity in Jewish music along with the entitlement of everyone who creates anything, no matter how elementary, to call themselves Jewish artists is the irony.

The resulting Jewish music today is the inevitable fruit of this democratized techno-artistic arena. At this juncture, with few exceptions, it is distinguished more for its parody of secular popular forms than by its original insight. But, as Rabbi Shalom Shakna ben Yosef posits in Buber's *Tales of the Hasidim*, "Good cannot come without opposition." Until the cream rises to the top, we must endure a prevailing, abounding, mediocrity both in thought and sound.

With the concomitant trivialization of theological ideas by pop culture, the quest for musical truth seems even more daunting. Meaning is not inherent; it is assigned. Through the conscious use of materials and design, the artist brings the willing audience on a journey of shared expression guided by signposts of delegated meaning. However, if the audience is not able or willing to fulfill this assignment, its odyssey being impeded by a lack of experience, language, training, or blind adherence to stylistic fashion, the artist's vision is stymied, diminished, incomplete, and, ultimately, unrealized.

It is very much like Moses on the mountaintop of Sinai receiving the law and envisioning the elevation of a Godly people, only to be suddenly amazed, shocked, and tragically heart broken at the lack of clarity and inability of the idolatrous Hebrews dancing below to a Golden Calf, failing to conceive of the awesome power just atop that small mountain of Sinai. After regrouping and praying for eighty days he comes down with the second tablets and offers it to but a few sympathetic souls who care and, indeed, are equipped to ascend to the same intellectual and emotional heights as their visionary leader.

Today's Jewish music songwriters tend to skirt the issue of elevated meaning both philosophically and stylistically rather than cull deeper musical possibilities from the *midrashic* potential of the message. There was a news report about a group that retold Torah stories in an urban – *hip hop* style. They touted their edgy humor and defended their narrative mockery by claiming, "A little bit of irreverence is very good in combating irrelevance."

Representing that the message of the Torah is either to be made irreverent or irrelevant to the present disaffiliated generation is, in itself, a philosophy that may be characterized as artistic *chutzpah* (gall). Unmistakably, there is a visible and discernible line between a theatrical point of view in the *Theatre of the Spirit* and a cross-over discounting of the value of traditional texts and messages for its own iconoclastic sake.

What is that difference? While one elevates the sacred from the mundane and separates the holy from the secular, the other, in an all too prevalent deconstructionist manner, pokes fun at icons and images employing secular and street parlance, simply because it is a post-adolescent, trendy, *Saturday Night Live* thing to do. It demeans rather than elevates, and secularly dilutes rather than separates. We are all the more impoverished for it.

High on the agenda of young adults in their twenties and early thirties is a need to be considered "new age," iconoclastic, and stylishly edgy to be attractive. The problem is that, with the current hyper-frequency in which musical ideas communicate, this "now" agenda, colored by an irreverent style with its concomitant lack of thoughtful *midrash,* emphasizes an indelible shallowness to a young generation, and the extended media network they attract, without the resonance of much accompanying insight and value.

The further adoption by fusion of world music styles like Reggae, Klezmer, (Slavic peasant music), and all forms of Latin sambas and Afro-pop or crossover ethnic borrowings from *Gospel* styles, avoids the more artful, introspective analysis of possible *midrashic* meanings for musical inspiration. While, undeniably, this music is divertingly entertaining, it is, inevitably, a retrogressive smokescreen that prevents clearer, more meaningful *midrashic* settings. This *B'nei Jeshurun* concept, named after the New York City Temple's Friday evening happening, which is currently all the rage, is yet another example of Deconstruction in our time.

In music for the synagogue, a *midrashic* ascent is also made more difficult by intermediary congregational leadership who lack experience and training to facilitate the elevation of this artistic communication. While it is obvious that cantors, serving as *sh'lichei tzibbur* (messengers of the congregation before God), need to be trained and able to fulfill their purpose, rabbis and temple boards need enriched musical training and experience as well, if they are to influence the sacred music that is being presented.

In the synagogue hierarchy of governance, the rabbi is given the authority to structure and fashion the worship service. Rabbis are trained to lead as *People of the Book.* They are literary and not necessarily musical. They receive no substantive seminary training in discerning and selecting the best musical settings of liturgy or life cycle rituals. If the rabbis have limited concert and/or recorded listening experience, their taste will simply be inadequate (or worse, embarrassing) for the task of making music policy for worship. Yet, their leadership imperatives often preclude thoughtful assignment of these crucial decision policies to the further detriment of their congregations.

Canadian synagogue music composer Ben Steinberg has written:

> There is an enormous difference between music as entertainment (acceptable in daily life), and sacred music as a language that teaches concepts, illuminates sacred texts and establishes moods for meaningful worship. When our sacred music adapts to these tasks with skill, knowledge, and especially with reference to centuries of tradition, our congregations are able to respond with seriousness, understanding and the mature pleasure, which can only result from an adult approach. This does not preclude congregational participation or joy in worship, but it does re-open the door to a multiplicity of beautiful musical styles that have been abandoned by large numbers of Jewish worship congregations.

> I recall that, when I was raised in the orthodox synagogue, we as children strove to learn in order that one day we might become educated, responsible adults. Today, it seems that many of our leaders are trying to turn us back into children.

In addition to rabbinic leadership, temple and synagogue board members also need musical training and experience. With more influence than ever, these laypersons increasingly dictate worship policy to both the cantor and the rabbi. Founded primarily on financial and time issues, temple boards often make the wrong choices based on their notions of immediate economy and shortening of the worship experience. They base their advice less on the larger picture or the bigger idea and react more to passing fads and monthly short falls. Until an insightful and balanced *bimah* is achieved – rabbi, cantor, and temple officials all striving for elevation first and expedience last — the prognosis for the elevation and advancement of synagogue music is discouraging at best.

However, there is a glimmer of hope. Our best rabbis are now sensing that dwindling attendance at services and decreased Jewish philanthropic activity calls for more than *musique du jour* fashionability. They are beginning, once again, to understand that the size of a congregation is also based on the size of the spirituality presented at services; the great idea of a great God calls for more than campfire music.

Here's how an insightful rabbi, Ed Feinstein, spiritual leader of Valley Beth Shalom Temple in Encino, California, addressed the issue of lack of philanthropic financial support in a Los Angeles Jewish Federation publication:

Welcoming the Prophets

By Rabbi Ed Feinstein

What percentage of charitable gifts in excess of a million dollars contributed by persons of Jewish origin during the past decade went to Jewish charities and causes?

According to a recent study, the answer is, only 5%. The remaining 95% went to universities, hospitals, symphony orchestras, art museums, charities and relief agencies – all worthy causes but unrelated to the Jewish community.

With all the needs of the Jewish community, why only 5%? Are these philanthropists markedly assimilated? Are they disillusioned with the Jewish community?

This accounts for part of the phenomenon. But according to the study's author, who interviewed several of the major donors, their principal reason was that the Jewish community presented no idea big enough to inspire a multi-million dollar gift. Where are our big ideas?

The Bible divides leadership among three personalities: The King is the executive, responsible for the management of the society. The King raises and distributes communal revenues, defends us against outside threats, and extends the community's domain. The Priest is the protector of collective.

The Priest preserves communal memory and tradition, inspires allegiance to the collective, and salves internal divisions. The Prophet is the conscience of the community and its source of vision. The Prophet calls upon the community to dream of new and truer expressions of its highest ideals. The Prophet raises the voice of protest whenever those ideals are transgressed.

The Prophet is an annoyance. Effective management demands constant compromise, but the Prophet is an absolutist who accepts and approves of no compromise. When we get it right, the Prophet reminds us that any moral triumph is only a momentary step in the direction of lofty dreams yet to be realized. In the Prophet's eyes, even our very best isn't ever good enough. The Prophet compels us to think bigger, see farther, dream mighty dreams, and accept nothing less than the best.

In the ancient history of Israel, Kings and Priests frequently united to silence the Prophet's voice. It is in their immediate interest to suppress the Prophet. But they ultimately do so at their peril, for without Prophets, vision dies. Without Prophets, the community loses its powers of moral imagination and its capacity to generate dreams. Without Prophets, the community's passion is extinguished.

In our Jewish community and it institutions, we have effective Kings and inspiring Priests, but who are our Prophets? Have we a community that welcomes the Prophetic voice and tolerates the Prophet's withering critique? Do we celebrate Prophetic visions or dismiss them as foolhardy? Who in our community is assigned the task of dreaming big dreams, big Jewish dreams?

For the past generation, our community has enjoyed a consensus about the issues that matter most. Despite all our differences, survival was everyone's number one priority. Survival meant fighting anti-Semitism, protecting Israel, welcoming immigrants and transmitting Judaism to the next generation. Survival is a holy purpose, particularly after the horrors of the Holocaust. But survival is a very conservative objective. We now face a generation asking, Survival for what purpose? Why survive? We can respond as the Priest, and dismiss the question as blasphemy.

Or we can invite the questioner into the community to sit with us and dream like Prophets. Know that there are millions of dollars, and millions of Jewish souls awaiting our answer.

The best Jewish music (music inspired by big ideas) serves as a *midrash* in our emotional connection to the *Tanach*, prayers, wisdom, and life-cycle moments just as much as words act as an intellectual commentary upon these texts and events.

How does music emotionally comment, clarify, and give context to the Jewish subject at hand? Our music achieves this by calling up associative memories, attractions, similarities, and seminal musical moments in our mind's audio files, providing us with a personal perspective and environment for comparing and contrasting and, ultimately, being touched emotionally, and affectively understanding the issue through these associations.

This musical *midrashic* understanding is non-verbal, intuitive, non-sequential, and a "right-brained" essential commentary.

•

Let me give you a musical example. When I composed *B'ni* for my son, Ari, the text dealt with a mature concept of not forsaking Torah and Jewish teachings. Most maturely, this might be taught to a son at Bar Mitzvah or at a later age to be fully fathomed and understood. However, emotionally, this was our hope for our son from the moment he was born. It was this image of the child in the cradle that prompted the synthesis of a tropal chant melody with an Alberti bass accompaniment in the style of a lullaby. When it was first performed, at Ari's baby naming, the image typified the aspirations of all new parents and, happily, the personal setting went on to enjoy a wide audience because of its emotional universality.

Other examples that come to mind are the multiple ways that I have set the *Sh'ma* in my sacred services. In my first camp setting *Avodat Amammit* it was a simple, youthful, lyrical call to attention. In *Hegyon Libi*, a string quartet service, it was a quiet, undulating, meditation culminating in the truth that *Adonai* is *One*. In *Nishmat Chayim*, a woodwind service, the image of the *Sh'ma* as a life preserver in a sea of doubts led to this heroic treatment, and in *L'maasei V'reisheet*, a children's millennial Shabbat service, I attach the preceding *Ahavat Olam* to the *Sh'ma*, as a concerted expression, to teach that only with great love for humanity and the world can we and our children ultimately hope to hear God's message and Israel's watchword.

Though it is the same *Sh'ma* text in all of these four circumstances it received contrasting levels of *midrashic* musical treatment in the PARDES, the musical garden of interpretation because of its inherent multi-leveled worlds of meaning.

•

I have written that Jewish music must be dramatic music for the *Theatre of the Spirit.* My background and concerted interests have always been in dramatic music, where I've provided scores for live theatrical events as well as for television and film. In all of these, I have been dedicated to providing musical subtexts to each drama. In the synagogue, the drama of our lives and our connection with God is the most compelling theatrical moment. What could be more visceral? If the music doesn't underscore this urgency to connect us to our Creator through love, awe, or basic need, I believe it is redundant to the literary impact of the words. If the words do the job, why add music?

It is the dramatic sub-text of emotion that musically completes the expression. In my setting of *Adonai Roi* I treat the 23rd psalm as a miniature three-act drama. Initially, we innocently enter life, optimistic and blithely confident that all is well. In the second act we walk through our *Valley of Shadows*, and, as we emerge in the third act, we triumph in our renewed and deeper, more mature understanding of God's spirit in our lives. Could there be better theatre than this?

Play recorded CD #34 — 23rd Psalm, sung by Cantor Faith Steinsnyder.

While all music should be engaging, sacred music should not merely theatrically entertain or excite us to mindless ecstasy, as it often does at the time of this writing. To fulfill truly its mission, the best sacred music needs to comment, offer a *midrash,* and underscore the "hidden message." We must understand and feel at the same time with both sides of our brain and our heart. It is simply not adequate for Jews to employ music to swoon. The wayward Israelites were swooners at the Golden Calf. We must do better, by thinking and feeling. To do less is to be less.

The best Jewish music (like all well-crafted music) lives simultaneously in three time dimensions. While being stylistically mindful (not fully reflective) of the present time in which it is written, it should also recall a knowingness of past traditions from which it formed its origins, and ultimately, by the originality of its setting, it should inspire alternative energies and creative musical directions to be explored into the future.

In order to serve its mission, past, present, and future dynamics must be organically interwoven into the fabric of these Jewish musical sounds and all the attendant arts in Judaism

This is why in *L'Maaseih V'reisheet – To Recreate the World*, the millennium-response Sabbath service that was commissioned by forty-three congregations throughout North America, I reset the Shabbat liturgy in both Hebrew and English, the instrumental style included the latest electronic synthesis, and the service was formatted on an accompaniment CD to enable smaller congregations to think as big as larger ones. I also used tropal chant, *nusach* and a feeling for *Misinai* settings. Past, present, and future dynamics all came into play.

Creating a cultural context in Judaism that elevates us demands that we rethink the concept of *Havdalah*, the separation of the sacred from the mundane. Today the *"Minhag America"* notion that we are all one has homogenized much of the way we think about and practice religion in general. However, Jews are not like everyone else and this separation has served to focus our mandate and distinguish our achievement.

Our generation will be remembered for knocking down barriers between genders, sexuality, mores, language, poetry, and art by borrowing from other religions and ideologies. While this iconoclasm has always been a Jewish tendency, it is also a two-sided coin in its long-term advantages and disadvantages. Eschewing a return to a *shtetl* (ghetto) mentality, if we do not maintain some sense of separation between what we see, hear, taste, touch, and sense inside our houses of worship from what we experience in our secular world, in short order they will all be of the same value. If this is so, Judaism will be interchangeable with any and every other belief, or worse, devalued to merely a secular occurrence.

Musically, I strive to elevate my sacred music and make it different in some way than the music I compose outside of the synagogue. This is becoming an increasingly unpopular strategy for those who believe that pious devotion is on an equal scale with "hipness." My Jewish music advocates a return to the separation of the sacred from the mundane and to a return to greatness not mere expedience.

Worship need not be relevant with other activities. It is special and apart. Relevance is a secular, temporal term. It is a style like fashion is *au courant*. While it may allude to the present, the real knack of a great worship service is to be timeless, transcending the mundane, the everyday, the *en vogue* sound *du jour*, and to create a *hevdeil*, a separation between what we know on earth and what we can imagine as being transcendent.

The more we endeavor to engage congregations through words and music that are primarily "of the time," "hip," and "with it," the more we miss the opportunity to elevate the service to an ethereal, timeless classicism. After hearing the most meaningfully effective prayer text or musical setting, does anyone care whether it was written yesterday or five hundred years ago? As Stefan Zweig noted in *World of Yesterday:*

"Great moments are always outside of time."

It is only the threatened insecurity of our Temple leaders who resort to the gimmick of a "happening" to address ineffectively what is not happening, transcendence within worship, which prolongs this policy.

•

Evaluating the Jewish music and art of our time, one can aver with great pride that we have come a long way. In the same breath, however, one must also say that we have not (even remotely) reached what we are capable of achieving. We are floating in a cloud, a smoke screen of the "feel-good" synagogue, holiday, and life cycle music that hides our loss of greater communal aspirations and identity.

Another lamentable but almost amusing trend in today's progressive reform, and even conservative worship liturgy, is the tendency to include pretentious, neo-Hassidic settings with a plethora of "ya la, lai's" replacing the actual Hebrew.

Think of it. In order to conjure up the meager but fabled authenticity of their grandparents and great grandparents, urban, 21st century reform Jews, who consider themselves contemporary in every other aspect of their *Minhag American* worship and Jewish lifestyle, suddenly regress to a faux *shtetilism* by singing "yuh bi bim bams, ay yai yais, and lai, lai, lai's" of their late 19th and early 20th century Pale-of-Settlement, *Fiddler-on-the-Roof* ancestors throughout the service. Is this not a classic musical case of buying into and being trapped by a Jewish Dybbuk (displaced soul in another's body) mentality?

One American reform cantor confided in me that she is now pressured so much to "lai, lai, lai" during every Sabbath setting that she has concluded, "There are now more lai's [lies] in our Friday evening Shabbat service than in politics!"

In spite of present musical realities that mirror a growing trivialization and discounting of religion's value in our lives, one must always conclude a *siyyum hasefer* (the conclusion of writing or studying a book) with hope and reaffirmation of belief. Life is that process of becoming closer to our Godliness. So, as author Lawrence Ferlinghetti waited for "the rebirth of freedom," in *Coney Island of the Mind*, I hope and compose for the rebirth of intelligent *midrash* in our Jewish music.

Here is a salient quote by the great Israeli Talmudic scholar Rabbi Adin Steinsaltz that closely exemplifies the essence of my involvement in Jewish music. He comments:

> There is a very short sentence: 'I am a Jew.' This short sentence has two possible melodies. One melody is: I have hemophilia, it's not my fault, but I got it. I'm sure not proud of it; in fact, I'd do whatever I could to get rid of it. The second melody is: I am a royal prince. I inherited it. It's not my fault, but I'm rather proud of it and I won't marry a commoner if I can avoid it. What I'm trying to do all my life is just to change the (first) melody, because the words can hardly be changed.

In the future, in addition to my own creative work, I look forward to a new generation of composers who are literate Hebraically, poetically, liturgically, and, above all, musically trained to appreciate the insight of those musical works by the finest composers and cantors who preceded them. Ultimately, I pray that these future prophets are asked to and are afforded the opportunities to use their creative skills, education, and energy in redefining and elevating future Jewish worship and the cycle of Jewish life in their moment on earth. Achieving this would surely go far in repairing our world.

•

"Hard as the world is to explain with the Almighty, it is harder yet without the Holy One."

—*Moses Montefiore (1784-1855)*

•